# DISCOVERING
# DRESSAGE

# CONTENTS

# INTRODUCTION

How often have you seen your horse moving effortlessly around the field in a powerful, extravagant extended trot and thought 'If only he would do that when I am on him'? Dressage aims to achieve this. It involves developing the horse's natural ability and training him to use his body in an efficient and athletic way, maintaining his balance at all times while carrying a rider.

As soon as you sit on a horse's back you alter his centre of gravity and upset his balance. He has total balance in his natural state, and it must be the rider's aim to restore this 'natural' balance and to help the horse achieve a total balance, or self-carriage, that incorporates the rider.

Even if you don't have ambitions to reach the height of Advanced dressage, learning the basics – the correct seat, the aids, the paces of the horse and some of the simple dressage movements – is fundamental to all riding activities. Dressage is the foundation of all other disciplines. A well-schooled horse is light and responsive to the aids, free and regular in his paces, supple and athletic in self-balance; above all, he is a pleasure to ride.

To the onlooker the picture should be one of elegance and ease, of horse and rider in perfect harmony. Developing harmony between horse and rider – obedience, balance, straightness and suppleness – will lead to better performance and greater potential in every sphere.

Laura Fry

# CHAPTER 1

# POSITION AND SEAT OF THE RIDER

The importance of a good seat is not to be underestimated. Without a correct and well-balanced position, you will not be able to apply the aids effectively and therefore cannot influence your horse as you would like. To ride effectively, your position must be so well established that you are able to give the horse precise aids and remain totally in balance with him as he responds to these aids. It takes many years of hard work to develop a correct and effective seat, so you must keep striving for perfection, even the most experienced rider continues to work on his seat.

There are several points to consider before starting work on your horse.

**A good seat is very important.**

## BALANCE

This is the ability to support and control your body weight and prevent it from hindering the horse in any way. Indeed, you must be able to assist the horse because you are going to teach him to achieve a degree of control that he would not attain in his natural free state.

Your balance will be developed through inner control rather than physical strength. In common with other activities, riding makes demands on muscles not regularly used in everyday life. It also requires you to relax various muscles that you use frequently but do not need for riding. You need to develop control over your muscles – this is a continuous process which will improve with time, constant practice and self-discipline.

## BREATHING

How you breathe is far more important than you might think. Irregular breathing, particularly the extreme of holding your breath, causes tension and stiffness in your body which will be conveyed to your horse; it will also tire you out. Try to breathe in a steady rhythm, relaxing as you breathe. Be careful not to stiffen or raise your shoulders, as this hinders your breathing.

## THE SADDLE

It is not essential to ride in a dressage saddle at this stage, but it is important that the saddle fits you and the horse. A dressage saddle generally has a deeper seat than a jumping saddle,

**A suitable saddle for dressage.**

with the stirrup bars only a little in front of the deepest part of the seat – this is to enable you to keep your legs underneath your centre of gravity and therefore to use them more effectively while maintaining an upright and elegant position.

A jumping saddle would bring your legs more in front of you because the stirrup bars are situated much further forward than the deepest part of the seat, with forward-cut flaps to accommodate your knees. This gives you a wider base of support and better balance while jumping, but would bring your legs too far forward for flatwork. If your only saddle is a jumping saddle, you will not find it as easy to achieve a good position for dressage. Lengthening your stirrup leathers will help, but you may still find that your lower leg is being dragged forward to where the stirrup hangs.

A general-purpose saddle enables

**A forward cut jumping saddle, unsuitable for dressage.**

you to do either flatwork or jumping fairly comfortably, though your stirrups need to be shorter for jumping and longer for dressage.

The stirrup leathers hang at right angles to the ground. If the saddle fits you and sits correctly on the horse's back, then you should find that when you sit in the deepest part of the saddle your legs will hang beneath your seat and the balls of your feet will sit comfortably on the stirrup irons without dragging the leathers either backwards or forwards.

## THE SEAT

The starting point of a correct seat is to find your two seat bones. Take your feet out of the stirrups and, keeping your back straight, lift both your knees up to the horse's withers; this takes the weight off your knees and thighs and concentrates it on your seat bones. Wriggle about until you

are sitting in the deepest part of the saddle. Now you should be able to feel if you have equal weight on each seat bone. If you are unsure, wriggle your bottom until you feel evenly supported.

Keeping your legs up, think now about your lower back. It should feel firm and supportive. Make sure that it is neither hollow nor round and that you are sitting up tall and straight; your shoulders should be directly above your hips.

You should not only be straight but also level – if you are doubtful, ask someone to check by standing directly behind you. Pay particular attention to your shoulders being level, as this will affect the way you hold and use the reins. If your shoulders are not at the same height as each other, recheck that your seat bones and hips are level; a fault in your upper body position often originates from an insecure or crooked seat. Your shoulders should be far enough back that your shoulder blades lie flat against the back of your rib cage – your shoulders should not appear rounded or hunched.

Keep your neck straight. It has to support your head, and *your* head carriage is just as important as your horse's. You need to keep your head up so that its weight is easily supported by your neck. Your ears should be directly above your shoulders. You should face straight ahead, although you may look about.

If your shoulders are in the correct position, each upper arm will fall comfortably against your side. Now bend your elbows, with your hands forward. Keep your elbows in to your sides but far enough forward that they are just ahead of your body. The

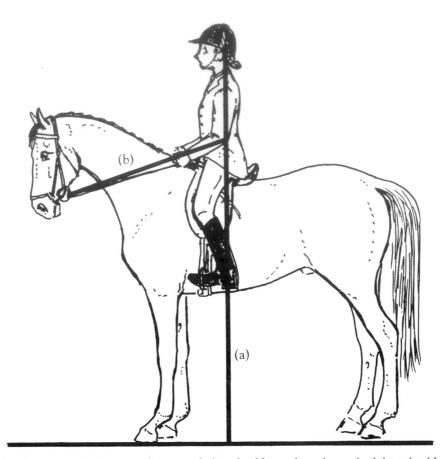

*(a) When you are sitting correctly, a straight line should pass through your heel, hip, shoulder and ear – this line should be at right angles to the ground.*
*(b) A straight line should also pass from your elbow, through your wrist and hand, straight down the rein to the bit.*

suppleness of your elbows is vital for the quality of the contact between your hands and the horse's mouth. Keep your elbows bent but very flexible so that you can always maintain a straight line from your elbow, through your forearm, wrist, hand and along the rein to the bit.

Having found the correct position for all of your upper body, try to maintain your upper body position while you correct your leg position.

Your knees should still be up by the horse's withers, so lift them away from the withers (holding the pommel of the saddle if you need to) and lower your legs until they are hanging easily against the horse's sides. Your knees should hang loosely so that your lower legs make cosy contact with the horse's sides. You should find that your heel now hangs directly below your hip.

While performing this exercise, take care that your back remains straight, supple and supportive and at a right angle to the ground. The line through your heel and hip will then also pass through your shoulder and straight up to your ear.

For your leg to be effective the heel must be lower than the toe. The action of lowering the heel makes the calf muscle firm and therefore enables you to give controlled leg aids, whereas raising the heel slackens the calf muscle causing floppy, unclear leg aids. Your toes should be pointing almost straight forward, allowing the inside of your lower leg to fall against the horse's side without tension.

You must be supple enough in your seat to accommodate the movement of the horse but secure enough not to lose your position. If you feel yourself becoming unbalanced or tense in some way, then stop and return to the basic principles.

ʊ   Carry your weight equally on each of your two seat bones.
ʊ   Keep your back upright and straight.
ʊ   Keep your neck and head upright, and look straight ahead.
ʊ   Your legs must hang freely from the hips, and stay close to the horse's side.

## HOLDING THE REINS

When you hold the reins, carry your hands in front of you with your thumbs on top and your fingers closed around the reins. The reins should pass between your last two fingers, then up through the palm of your hand and out over your first finger, under your thumb.

*How to hold the reins.*

## STIRRUP LENGTH

The correct length of stirrup depends not only on your shape and size, but also on the shape, size and balance of your horse. As a very rough guide, when your legs hang at their longest and without your feet in the stirrups, the bottom of the iron should be level with your ankle bone.

Beware of having your stirrups too long: it will upset your balance far more than if they are too short. I have seen many small riders who think that they can make up for their lack of height by riding with long stirrups. They lose their balance through having to straighten their knees and point their toes downwards to reach

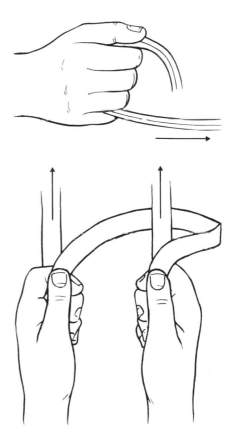

for the stirrups. This in turn brings the weight off the seat bones and on to the fork, thus upsetting the balance of both horse and rider, tipping both on to the forehand. It is important that your weight is spread evenly over the ball of your foot and that more weight goes down into your heel than into your toe.

## THE LUNGE LESSON

The best way to improve your riding position is on the lunge, because the horse will be under the full control of someone else, allowing you to concentrate on your position. Try to find an experienced instructor who will control the horse and at the same time help you to develop a good position. If you can't find an instructor, however, anyone who can lunge your horse well enough for you to be able to think solely about your position will be a help.

Your horse must be accustomed to lungeing because you will need to do some exercises to improve your suppleness, and he must not mind this. He will need to work in side reins, which will help him maintain a steady rhythm, balance and outline, and give the instructor better control – leaving you free to work on keeping your balance and on achieving, controlling and maintaining a steady position.

The lunge lesson should always start with the horse being loosened up without you on him. If he is quiet and accepts the side reins, then you can very soon mount. *Always* undo the side reins prior to mounting, then refasten them before you move off. When you are mounted and comfortable, the instructor should

check that your seat is correct in the halt – once the horse starts to move you will have to concentrate on following his movement.

### Exercises

Exercises on the lunge can make you more supple and better balanced. Try the following.

1 **Head and neck** (a) Turn your head slowly 90 degrees to the left and right. (b) Roll your head in a circle, forward, sideways, back, sideways – clockwise and anti-clockwise. (c) Tip your head back until your neck rests against your collar, then drop your chin to the normal position, keeping your neck well back into your collar.

2 **Shoulders and arms** (a) Shrug your shoulders slowly, as high as you can, then let them drop down and back; repeat this several times. (b) Lift one arm and stretch it right up above your head, then circle it slowly backwards several times; repeat with the other arm. (c) Circle left and right arms backwards alternately, then try circling both together very slowly.

3 **Waist** (a) Hold your arms straight out to the side at shoulder height, then twist from your waist 90 degrees to left and right alternately, keeping your arms level and straight, and your legs still. (b) Do the same exercise with your hands on your hips, not out to the sides. (c) Bend at your waist and touch your toes on each side, but be careful to keep your legs still.

4 **Legs** (a) Wriggle your toes inside your boots. (b) Circle your feet clockwise and anti-clockwise (up, out, down, in, down, out, up). (c) Swing your lower legs, from the knee, one backwards and one fowards, changing direction alternately. (d) Swing your whole leg, from the hip, one forwards

and one backwards, alternately. (e) Lift your knees away from the saddle, hold them still for a second, then let them fall gently back on to the saddle; repeat several times.

These exercises can be repeated several times in walk. When you find them easy, some can be performed in trot – 2(b) and (c), 3(a) and (b), and all of 4. As your balance and suppleness improve, you will find the exercises easier and can then increase the number of each that you do. You should work both sides of your body equally, and change direction frequently during the lunge lesson.

## Developing a sixth sense

At the end of the lunge lesson you should begin to feel what is correct, so that if you start to lose your position as you go on to schooling your horse you will know at once and can put it right. This matter of 'feel' is very, very important. It is the sixth sense that comes from much concentration and hard work, a sixth sense which will tell you when things are right and when they are going wrong.

'Feel' comes from learning how to develop your mind as well as learning how to use your body. A thinking rider who gives his horse his full concentration at all times when riding will often develop into a better rider than one who is naturally talented but lacks the necessary dedication and self-discipline. It is easy to fall into bad habits when riding – a fault in your riding position is much more likely to become a habit if your concentration is poor and you therefore fail to correct it soon enough.

### Riding without stirrups

Riding without your stirrups for frequent, short periods will help you to develop a deeper seat and better balance. It can be done either on the lunge or when riding loose. The advantage of a deeper seat is that you can follow the movement of the horse with greater ease and therefore will be less hindrance to him; you can also apply the aids with more precision. As you develop the balance and correctness of your seat, you will be able to refine your aids until they are hardly noticeable to the onlooker, thus creating a picture of harmony and ease which should be the aim of every rider.

# CHAPTER 2

# THE AIDS

To make your horse a pleasure to ride you have to teach him to be obedient. Obedience stems from understanding, trust and respect. Understanding and trust are achieved through consistency and praise; respect is gained through correction and repetition.

You can talk directly to the horse – the aids are the language you use. They are the means by which you control the horse, and the signals or instructions you give him. There are two types of aids the *natural aids* (your seat, legs, hands and voice) and the *artificial aids* (whip and spurs).

If the language of the aids is clear and simple the horse will understand; if it is complicated and difficult the horse will be confused. For the aids to be clear and simple you must be balanced and have a 'feel' for the horse. In addition, you must give the aids while maintaining a good and secure position; this will have been developed by work on the lunge.

When you can give good aids and feel your horse's reaction to them, you will be able to develop better communication between yourself and your horse. Training a horse is a lengthy process, so the sooner that you and he learn to communicate the sooner that serious training can begin. Always remember that your horse is far bigger and stronger than you, therefore any attempt to force him to do something is not only futile, but will almost certainly force him out of balance. Instead, he must be taught to understand, which you do by repeating an aid until he responds to it, then by praising him.

Teaching your horse to halt from walk provides a good example of how you use repetition and praise. First sit tall, close your lower legs and push him into a restraining (but not restricting) rein. If he doesn't respond, release the aids momentarily and then reapply them slightly more strongly. If he still doesn't respond, release them again momentarily and then reapply them, again a little more strongly. Repeat again if necessary until he halts – then immediately relax your aids and praise him. Remain in the halt until he stands quietly. If he moves again before you are ready, reapply the aids and repeat as before.

Repeat the transition several times until he responds immediately to your aids. It is a good idea to ask for the halt every time at the same place – the horse will understand more easily and will therefore eagerly await the next aid. Once the horse has understood and can respond quickly to this aid, gradually refine it until you can achieve a halt from the lightest of aids.

# THE NATURAL AIDS

Although each of the aids is discussed separately here, they are not used in isolation but together. Remember: clear, simple aids used consistently are the basis of the horse's understanding, trust and respect.

## *The seat*

Chapter 1 explains how to attain the right seat for dressage. The seat is used in conjunction with the legs to ask the horse to move forwards or sideways or to create more activity and impulsion and help maintain balance.

## *The legs*

The rider's legs are used either 'passively' (lightly closed just behind the girth) to keep the horse moving forwards in a straight line, or 'actively' (by giving little taps) to ask for more forward movement. Imagine trying to hammer a small nail into a wall by leaning the hammer on the head of the nail and pressing – nothing will happen. However, if you take the hammer a little way back from the nail then give it several little taps, you will succeed. Similarly, when asking your horse to move forwards you must ask with a moving leg, but not by squeezing and gripping. The legs are also used to slow down, by closing them to restrain the forward movement; and they are used to bend the horse, by pressing the leg on the girth on the side to which you want the horse to bend.

**The rider is working under instruction on the lunge to improve her position. A good leg position will enable her to give clear leg aids. On the left her lower legs are not in contact with the horse's sides and will not be able to give effective aids, but in the photograph on the right she has corrected this.**

## The hands

The rider's hands convey messages to the horse's mouth via the reins. Hands should be so much a part of the reins that these aids can be called rein aids. The rein aids should always be used in conjunction with leg and seat aids.

If you maintain a steady and elastic contact with the horse's mouth at all times, then you will be able to give light and precise rein aids. If, however, you use the reins to keep your balance or to hold yourself in the saddle then the horse will not know which of your movements he should respond to and which he should not. He will either become numb in the mouth and 'dead' to all your rein aids, or he will 'drop the bit' and refuse to take any contact at all. It is vital that you don't abuse the horse's mouth because you will need his confidence in the contact to control him.

Your hands must be able to move independently from your body and they must be independent from each other.

## The voice

The voice is used from the very beginning of a horse's education – first when he is a foal and then during handling as a young horse. It is useful for soothing a worried horse and for praising. If voice aids are clearly understood from an early age, then they can be used in conjunction with the seat, legs and hands when the horse is first ridden until he learns to respond to these.

Voice aids should be precise and clear. 'Will you please trot' means nothing – but 't-e-r-r-rot' said energetically as two syllables would be clearer for a horse to understand as a forward aid. For decreasing pace a more soothing tone should be used, with the second syllable in a lower (rather than higher) tone, like 'waa-alk'. Words must be simple; the tone is important as is the energy conveyed in your voice.

## THE ARTIFICIAL AIDS

The artificial aids are used to reinforce the natural aids when necessary but they should *never* be used instead of the natural aids, *never* with physical force and *never* in anger or frustration.

The whip is useful to reinforce a leg aid which has not produced a good reaction. It can be carried unobtrusively and used when necessary by giving a short flick just behind your leg. When your horse reacts correctly to this, praise him immediately so that he understands why you have used it. A dressage whip is longer than an ordinary whip so that it can be used just behind the leg without moving your hand from the reins or disturbing the contact with your horse's mouth. (The use of the whip is covered on p. 23.)

The spurs are used in the same way as the whip to improve your horse's reaction to your leg aids until eventually you can achieve the same reaction from the lightest of aids. This process of refining the aids should continue throughout the training of your horse. Before using spurs you must have established a correct position and have total control over your legs so that you will never touch the horse with them unintentionally.

Spurs are compulsory in Medium and Advanced competitions. Whips are permitted other than in championships or selection competitions.

Not permitted under any rules is the use of running reins. These are an artificial aid which can be used successfully by experienced riders to overcome training problems, but unless you understand exactly why and how to use them they are not to be recommended and could cause much damage.

There are no short cuts or substitutes for correct and careful training. Too much use of artifical aids will make the horse less respectful of the natural aids.

# CHAPTER 3

# PREPARATION FOR SCHOOLING

Before you can actually start schooling, there are three things to consider: the place to school, the equipment to use and the plan.

## THE PLACE

If you are lucky enough to have an all-weather arena or an indoor school near you, then that is the ideal place to work. If you have a field that you can use, then find an area approximately 40m (44yd)×20m (22yd) that is relatively flat and even. Mark out the corners of the rectangle with cones or something that you will see clearly when mounted, then mark the middle of each long side. If you have enough markers, you can also mark A, C, M, F, K and H (see diagram).

A short arena is sufficient for your work to start with. It is the size that is used for most dressage tests up to Medium level. The long arena is used for the more advanced tests and can be useful when teaching a young horse to lengthen his stride – a larger arena will encourage him to go more freely forwards.

However, if you do not have access to a suitable field or area to work in, then you must begin your schooling while you are hacking. The first lessons of obedience can be learned

just as easily in this way, and it will also be possible to work on simple transitions, rhythm, balance and outline. When you want to start riding some basic movements and lateral work (see Chapters 9 and 10), then it will be necessary to seek out a local arena or field that you can hire or borrow once or twice a week.

## THE EQUIPMENT

### For the rider

The equipment you need for basic dressage is practically the same as for general riding unless you decide to get a dressage saddle. As with all riding, your *hat* is the most important thing to wear at all times. It should have a proper chin strap and comply with the current British Standards.

A proper pair of *riding boots* is essential. Jodhpur boots are quite acceptable for children but it is surprising how much easier it is to keep your legs still in long boots. I like to see adult and teenage riders in long boots – wobbly lower legs, especially at the ankles, can only give wobbly aids. Boots which slip down and constantly have to be pulled up are very frustrating, so it really is worth seeking out a good pair. *Breeches or jodhpurs* are not vital but will be much more comfortable than jeans or

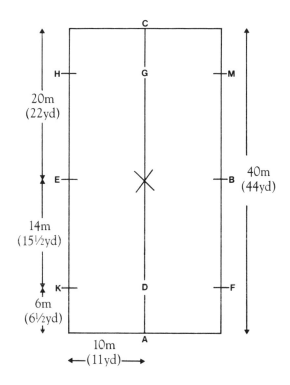

*A short arena (20 × 40 metres).*

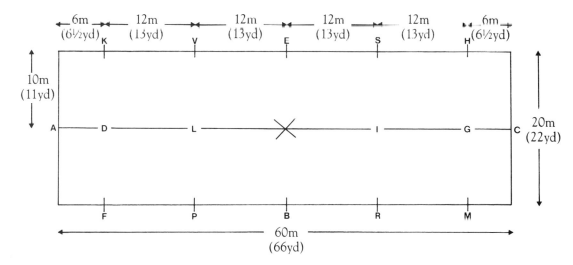

*A long arena (20 × 60 metres).*

trousers. When you are trying to improve your seat you will encounter enough problems without hindering yourself with uncomfortable clothes that pinch or wrinkle.

*Riding gloves*, to me, are absolutely essential. They need not be expensive (although leather ones are nice!). I find that gloves enable me to keep my fingers closed around the reins for long periods if necessary, without becoming sore. If your horse is strong and keen to run away, then gloves will give you a better grip on the reins.

Also, bear in mind what you will have to wear in a dressage competition. It is easier if you are used to being correctly dressed – there are enough difficulties to overcome when you compete, without the added discomfort of unfamiliar clothing.

## For the horse

The *saddle* was discussed on p. 8. The most important requirement is that it fits the horse and enables you to sit correctly. Some dressage saddles have long girth straps so that the buckles are low down to allow the closest possible contact between your legs and the horse. This is by no means essential, but it helps, and it is quite simple on any saddle to replace short straps with long ones.

I always use a thin *numnah* under the saddle because I think it is more comfortable for the horse and protects the underneath of the saddle. Make sure that the numnah is bigger than the saddle and well-secured so that it can't slip and rub the horse's back. If the numnah is too thick, the extra bulk between your upper legs and the horse may push your lower legs away from the horse's side.

**A numnah and sponge pad under the saddle are comfortable for the horse**.

A *sponge* or *gel 'pad'* can be used as well as a numnah if the horse has a sensitive back. This fits under the seat of the saddle and acts as a cushion between horse and rider. I find it useful because it gives you more padding under the seat where it is needed most, without making a thick bulge under your leg.

The *bridle* should be as simple as possible. Don't make any sudden changes or you may find yourself out of control! A snaffle is a good bit for schooling and there are many different ones to choose from; it is

**A loose ring bit.**

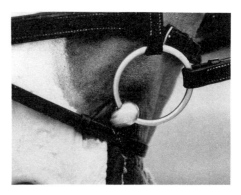

very important that the bit fits your horse's mouth, not only in width but also in thickness. A small-mouthed horse with a fat tongue will be happier with less ironmongery in his mouth.

A loose ring bit allows more movement of the bit within the horse's mouth and will often encourage a horse with a dry or 'dead' mouth to chomp the bit and relax his jaw. A fixed ring bit stays stiller in the horse's mouth.

The reins are important, too. Use reins that fit your hands comfortably. If they are too wide your fingers will not be able to close around them; if they are too narrow your hands will be clenched to stop them slipping. There is nothing more frustrating than reins which keep slipping through your fingers – if this happens

**Brushing boots protect the horse's legs.**

**A fixed ring bit.**

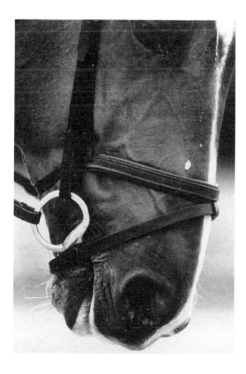

to you, try using rubber-covered reins, which are easy to hold even in the rain. Be sure to keep your left and right reins the same length all the time. Try sticking a piece of tape around each rein just ahead of where your hands would be in trot, then you can see at a glance whether they are equal when you're riding.

'Gadgets' are not allowed in dressage competitions, so if you plan to compete it is better not to use them at home either. Try gradually loosening a martingale so that it will still be effective in emergency but does not interfere with the bit too much.

I always use *brushing boots* when I am schooling. These will protect the horse's legs if he knocks himself, which he may do especially if he is young, unbalanced and not always on your aids.

*Whip held correctly, and a good length – the contact point is just behind the rider's leg.*

*Whip held incorrectly – waving about in the air. This is unattractive and useless.*

## Artificial aids

You shouldn't need spurs at the beginning but a *schooling* or *dressage whip* would be useful, provided that your horse is not whip-shy. The whip should be long enough to enable you to touch the horse just behind your leg with a slight turn of the wrist; if you have to disturb your hand position to use the whip, then it is too short. In the same way the whip must not touch the horse unintentionally, which may happen if the whip is too long or too bendy – a firm whip is easier to control. A whip with a knob on the top is easier to hold because it will not slip through your fingers.

Carry the whip so that it lies across your leg just above the knee. That way it will be easy to use to reinforce your leg and should not interfere with the rein contact. It is not uncommon to see the whip held so that it points above the horse's back, waving in the air – this is totally ineffective as it not only looks awful, but it cannot be used to reinforce the leg from this angle, without moving the hand and upsetting the contact.

The whip is most often used in the inside hand, but either hand will do. It is distracting for you and the horse if you change the whip into your inside hand every time you change direction. When you have discovered which leg your horse responds to least well, then carry the whip in that hand.

## THE PLAN

Before you rush out to school your horse, first decide how much you can reasonably expect from him. Take into account the following factors.

ʊ *His age* An old horse may need a longer time to loosen up, while a younger horse may have a shorter concentration span.

ʊ *How fit he is* A very fit horse may not settle in walk at the beginning. It is better to let him burn off some of his energy in a slow trot than to have to fight to make him walk. An unfit horse will need to do more in walk.

ʊ *His temperament* How much will he be able to take in, in one schooling sesson? It is better to ask only a little of him to begin with than to rush ahead and risk destroying his confidence – remember that he should enjoy his work. If he is very lazy the first priority must be to make him more willing to go forwards. If he is inattentive and disobedient, the first priority must be obedience.

ʊ *His conformation* A well-balanced horse will make quicker progress.

Decide what you will aim to achieve. For example, with an excitable, forward-going horse, the first few sessions must be spent developing confidence and trust in the partnership, and making sure that you are in control. Beware of trying to relax the horse by 'doing nothing'; most horses will find security in a steady leg and rein contact. You must accustom him to simple aids by working quietly through transitions between walk and trot. Try to find a steady rhythm in his paces – don't hurry him forwards.

The work period consists of three sections: first warming up; next, a period of constructive work which includes confirming what has already been taught and then teaching new things; and, finally, a cooling-off period. The first and last sections are just as important as the second.

In the warming-up period, you should begin by walking on a long rein, allowing the horse to stretch his neck forward and down and encouraging him to walk freely forwards. He cannot be expected to come out of the stable where he might have been standing still for 23 hours and start working hard immediately. No athlete would attempt a sprint until he was fully warmed up – he would risk injury to muscles.

When you have walked on a long rein for five to ten minutes, start some easy trot work. Allow the horse to stretch his neck downwards if he would like to but not upwards or inattentively. Trot for several minutes, making large circles and smooth changes of direction. Some horses benefit from a bit of canterwork at this stage, but if canter tends to excite him, leave it until later. Now give him a short walk to recover his breath. If you feel that he is well loosened-up, you can start on your proper work now. If you feel that he is particularly stiff, however, carry on with your warming-up exercises until he improves. We all have days when we feel incapable of being relaxed and supple – horses are the same, so do not be too impatient. There may be some days when all the time that you have available to ride is taken up by warming up and cooling off, so be patient.

At the end of a schooling session, walk on a long rein until the horse is absolutely cool, dry and breathing normally. He should return to his stable or field feeling comfortable, relaxed and supple. Always leave enough time to cool off.

I am often asked, 'how often do you school your horse, and for how long?' There is, of course, no set rule for this. A lot depends on your ability to concentrate and on what you are trying to achieve. Once a rider starts to tire, he rides less and less well. Push yourself hard but try to finish on a high note for both yourself and the horse, before either of you becomes exhausted. I find that the only time a horse gets bored or stale due to a lot of schooling is when the rider is bored, and rides aimlessly in circles without making any improvement. If you have no inclination to make your schooling productive, then there is no point in schooling at all.

I think that horses should be educated in as many ways as possible to give them a broader outlook on life – for example, by hacking, pole and grid work, jumping and schooling in different places. This makes them alert and keen and keeps them interested.

To reach a high level in dressage, a lot of hard work is required. Five sessions per week will get you there sooner than one or two. Several shorter sessions per week are better than one very long one; these can be followed by a hack or jumping session if you like.

CHAPTER 4

# THE PACES OF THE HORSE

To understand how to work your horse, you must be familiar with how he moves and with his paces, so that you can work on developing his natural ability. No two horses move in exactly the same way, but if you school your horse to develop his rhythm, his balance and his suppleness, you will teach him how best to use his body and show his paces at their best.

The paces of a horse are the different 'gaits' in which he moves. We can walk or run but, because a horse has four legs where we have only two, he can not only walk and run (trot) but also canter and gallop. When we have learned to walk and run we can then learn to hop, jump, skip and run sideways or backwards – but these cannot be kept up for long and require more balance than a walk or a run. In the same way, a horse must first learn to balance himself in walk, trot and canter before he can move on to the more difficult dressage movements such as half-pass and flying changes.

The gallop is the only pace which is not used in dressage (even though horses have occasionally been seen leaving the competition arena at a gallop either during or after their tests against their riders' wishes!).

Changes from one gait to another (for example, walk to trot) are known

as transitions. The aids for these are described in detail in Chapter 6. Changes between collected, working, medium and extended paces are also transitions, but this work is more advanced.

## THE WALK

The walk is a four-time pace, which means that there are four beats to every stride. The horse moves his four legs independently, but the footfalls are in a regular sequence and the time between each footfall should be the same. The sequence of the footfalls is: near hind, near fore, off hind, off fore. Learn to feel the movement of each step in walk. If you find it difficult to pick up the four beats of the walk while schooling, try listening for them when you ride on the road; you should hear four clear regular beats. When you have this rhythm in mind try to feel which of your horse's legs is moving for each beat.

To follow the horse's movement in walk you must be relaxed but not floppy, allowing the horse to move you. Your hands must follow the movement of his head and neck with a light contact, not restricting him in any way. Keep your legs lightly against his sides – you shouldn't need to nag constantly to make him walk forwards. A light touch with the whip can be used to back up the leg aid if necessary.

If your horse likes to hurry the walk, do not try to hold him at the right speed. Check his speed almost to a stop, then allow with your hand (lighten the pressure on the reins) and use your leg to push him forwards to the right speed. Repeat this as necessary until he understands that your leg is asking him to walk forwards into a light rein contact but not to hurry or to pull.

There is no moment of suspension in the walk – at least one foot is always on the ground. The horse steps from foot to foot, in contrast to the trot, where he springs from foot to foot with a moment of suspension when all four feet are off the ground. The length of stride at walk is less flexible than at trot owing to this. Compare the difference between shortening and lengthening your own stride at a walk or at a run. You will find that, while running, you are able to run almost on the spot and you are able to sprint, whereas in walk your steps become stilted if too short, and unbalanced if too long.

### Types of Walk

There are four types of walk: free, medium, extended and collected. You should learn them in that order.

The *free* walk is the most basic. It is usually ridden on a long rein with the horse stretching his neck well forwards into a light passive contact. The steps should be free and regular, and the hindfeet should overtrack the prints of the forefeet.

In *medium* walk the energy should be more contained and the horse ridden into a rounder outline on the

bit (see Chapter 5). This is achieved through half-halts (see p.44) until the horse is 'between hand and leg' – active, alert and ready for whatever may be asked for next.

The *extended* walk has the longest possible strides, with the hind feet overtracking well and with plenty of activity swinging forwards through the whole body of the horse into a longer but still round outline.

In *collected* walk the steps are shorter, but higher and more rounded. This requires greater engagement of the hocks. The hind feet will not overtrack the forefeet in collected walk, and the energy will be contained more upwards and less forwards, with the neck raised and arched.

It is very easy to spoil a horse's walk by pushing him out of his rhythm and out of balance. His walk may

*The steps in collected walk.*

*The steps in medium walk.*

*The steps in free walk.*

*The steps in extended walk.*

*The steps in collected, medium, free and extended walk; notice how the shape of the steps varies from short and elevated in collected walk to long and ground-covering but less elevated in extended walk.*

eventually become 'broken' and lose the correct sequence of footfalls, becoming a two-time pace with the near hind and near fore moving together and the off hind and off fore moving together. This incorrect walk is called 'pacing', and is severely marked down in dressage. Rider interference is at the root of the most common causes of pacing. These include over-shortening, hurrying, and the rider's hands being too strong or fiddling against the horse's mouth, causing him to stiffen his neck and back and to lose his true movement.

The paces are said to be 'true' when they are correct and natural. To keep the walk true do not be too demanding, but allow the horse to stretch his neck and relax into his own rhythm.

## THE TROT

The trot is a two-time pace; the horse moves his legs in diagonal pairs with a moment of suspension in between. The near hind and off fore move together, and the off hind and near fore move together. The action of the hind legs should match that of the forelegs, and the hind feet should come well into the prints of the forefeet.

As a horse's training progresses towards collection, the steps will become higher and rounder, covering less ground forwards but spending longer above the ground. There will be greater flexibility in the knee and hock joints. The moment of suspension will become more pronounced as the horse springs higher off the ground, leading ultimately to 'passage', the highly elevated trot performed only

at advanced level.

When working the novice horse in trot, the first priority is to achieve a true and regular trot, moving freely forwards in a steady rhythm. Some horses will naturally have a better trot than others. Some will have a natural rhythm while others will tend to take hurried, uneven steps.

To find your horse's rhythm, slow him right down almost to a walk, then use your leg to push him forwards again, feeling for the two beats of each stride. If you go too slowly he will lose the moment of suspension in his trot and will 'step' from diagonal to diagonal. If you go too fast, he will lose the suspension by flattening his stride and scuffling from diagonal to diagonal. At the correct speed he will have enough forward momentum to lift him off the ground and enough time between each stride to *keep* him off the ground for the moment of suspension. Listening to his hoof beats in trot, you should hear 1.2.1.2.1.2.1.2.

### Rising trot and sitting trot
The trot can be ridden either rising or sitting. The *rising* trot should always be used at the beginning of your schooling session. It allows the horse more freedom in his back because your weight is carried by your legs rather than your seat. The horse should not be expected to carry your sitting weight until he is warmed up and relaxed in his back. In the *sitting* trot you sit evenly through every stride. This often makes it easier to feel the quality of the trot. If your position is not secure, however, you will bump on your horse's back and he will stiffen his back against you, thus spoiling the quality of the trot.

It is important to keep your leg aids the same in sitting and in rising trot. It is common to see riders in rising trot who close their legs as they sit and open them as they rise – or vice-versa. You should not have to push the horse at every stride that is, when you rise *and* when you sit. Beware, however, of pushing the horse every other stride – that is, *only* when you sit or when you rise. This would tell one diagonal pair of the horse's legs to move with more energy, but the other diagonal pair would receive no messages at all. So keep your legs close to the horse at all times; use your legs when you need to create more energy but do *not* flap them on and off in the rhythm of the trot.

Rising trot may appear to be easier than sitting trot, but it is just as important to sit correctly when you rise as when you sit. It is unattractive and uncomfortable for the horse if you exaggerate the rise and the sit – thrusting your seat out of the saddle. Remember that it is your *legs* that drive the horse in rising trot, not your seat. Trying to use your seat to create more energy by rising higher and faster and bouncing heavily into the saddle will only make the horse stiffen his back against you. Allow your seat to rise slowly out of the saddle and then to sink slowly back down to the saddle, landing gently.

Your legs and hands should remain as still as possible in the rising trot. Your elbows must be very flexible, bending more when you sit and less when you rise. This will ensure that your hands follow the contact with the horse's mouth, rather than following your body up and down.

In Preliminary and Novice dressage, either rising or sitting trot is allowed, but from Elementary level upwards sitting trot is compulsory, as this gives the rider greater influence over his horse with his seat.

## Diagonals

In rising trot, you sit when one diagonal pair of legs comes to the ground (for one beat) and you rise off the horse's back when the other diagonal comes to the ground (for one beat). There are two alternatives: either sitting when the near fore and off hind come to the ground or sitting when the off fore and near hind come to the ground.

It may be difficult at first to know which diagonal you are on, but try not to look down at the horse's legs or you will unbalance him! It is usually possible to see by the movement of his shoulders which leg is on the ground. If you are confused, go into sitting trot on the left rein, and try to feel the movement of his forelegs. Actually say aloud, 'Left. right. left. right' with each stride. When this is firmly in your mind, translate the 'left' to 'rise' and 'right' to 'sit'. When you are confident with saying, 'rise-sit' then join in with your body.

When hacking, you should take care to 'change' diagonals regularly – to do this, sit for two beats instead of one. Some riders find one diagonal more comfortable than the other, and so do some horses; *never* allow your horse or yourself to favour a particular diagonal. While schooling you should sit when the inside hind leg and outside foreleg come to the ground and rise when the outside hind leg and inside foreleg come to the ground.

Each time you change direction you

In working trot, the horse moves actively forwards in a round outline.

Lengthened strides in trot. Notice how the horse straightens and stretches his foreleg before it touches the ground and brings his hind leg well under his body.

**A well balanced medium trot.**

must change your diagonal. Although this is important, try to do it at a place where it will not unbalance you or the horse. Do not do it in the middle of lengthened strides across the diagonal – wait until you reach the corner.

## Types of trot

There are four types of trot: working, medium, collected and extended.

The *working* trot is the basic trot and is just what it sounds – working. The horse must move actively forwards, making good use of his hind legs to create energy from behind, enabling him to move through his back in free, regular strides. His outline should be round, with a light but steady rein contact. In Novice dressage tests, the horse has to show

some 'lengthened strides' from the working trot. These are required only for a short distance and can be progressive, to ensure that the horse maintains his balance. When the horse develops greater engagement of his hind legs and can work more towards collection, he will be able to lengthen for longer distances and more easily. This will be the start of his medium trot.

In *medium* trot the strides are longer than in working trot and the horse covers more ground without altering his rhythm. He should lengthen his frame, which can only be performed satisfactorily if he is truly carrying himself, not relying on the rider's hands to hold him up in front. The front feet should touch the ground at the spot where they are pointing. If his toes 'flick' towards a point beyond where they will actually land this is incorrect. It usually means that the horse is unbalanced and too much on his forehand. Being unable to swing through his shoulders to produce a true medium trot, he compensates by flicking his toes to make the strides longer. This may look an attractive picture at first sight, but with a closer look you will notice that the hind legs are not as active as the forelegs. The cannon bones of the foreleg and hind leg in each diagonal pair must be at the same angle.

In *collected* trot, the horse bends his hocks more and his hind legs step further under his body, carrying more of his weight. This makes his forehand lighter and allows greater freedom in his shoulders, enabling him to take higher, more rounded steps. His neck should be raised and arched (owing to better balance not to the rider physically pulling his head up). The collected trot steps cover less ground than working trot, but the moment of suspension is more pronounced. Because of the greater degree of balance and control, the collected trot is used for lateral work such as shoulder-in and half-pass, which are discussed in Chapter 10.

The development of the *extended* trot results from a greater degree of lengthening – which in turn is the result of the greater degree of balance achieved in the collected trot. For this the horse lengthens his strides and frame even more than in the medium trot, stretching himself but still maintaining a high degree of balance and self-carriage. The moment of suspension is prolonged, and at this

*Strides in collected trot.*

*Strides in working trot.*

*Strides in medium trot.*

*Strides in extended trot.*

*The strides in collected, working, medium and extended trot; again notice the shape of the steps.*

point some horses appear hardly to touch the ground at all, being so light on their feet. Although in an extended frame, the horse still remains steady on the bit with a light, elastic contact.

## THE CANTER

The canter is a three-time pace, which means that there are three beats to every stride. One diagonal pair of the horse's legs move together to form one beat and the other two legs move separately to form the other two beats of the stride. There is a moment of suspension between each stride. Because of the three-beat stride in canter, there are two sequences of footfalls. One is for right canter – 1 (near hind) 2 (off hind and near fore) 3 (off fore); and one is for left canter – 1 (off hind) 2 (near hind and off fore) 3 (near fore).

The transition to canter is called the 'strike-off'. It is very important that horse and rider learn the correct aids

**An expressive canter, clearly showing the moment of suspension.**

for the strike-off to left canter and to right canter. A muddled strike-off produces a poor canter. The horse should never be made to trot faster and faster until he finally breaks into a canter – the rhythm of his trot should not alter before the strike off.

If the horse is cantering in an arena or on a circle, he will be better balanced if he canters 'on the correct leg'. This means cantering in the correct sequence of footfalls, with the inside foreleg making the last beat of every stride and the outside hind making the first beat. This is called 'true canter', and the inside foreleg is said to be 'leading' (making the last beat of each stride).

The horse is 'on the wrong leg' if his outside foreleg is 'leading'. Some

horses find it much easier to canter on one leg than the other. They may even find a circle easier on the wrong leg one way, but this can be corrected with patient schooling.

When the horse is well-balanced in both canter left and right, he will be able to learn 'counter canter' which is deliberately being 'on the wrong leg'. Rider and horse need to be very well-balanced for this and the horse must be obedient.

When the canter steps are in the correct sequence, 1 (outside hind) 2 (inside hind and outside fore) 3 (inside fore) the canter is 'united'.

Sometimes the sequence can become muddled. This might happen when the horse is unbalanced and changes legs behind but not in front.

The best way to improve your position and balance is on the lunge, with an instructor who controls the horse and helps you to develop your seat.

Horse and rider suitably turned out for a schooling session.

**Medium canter.**

**Extended canter.**

**Deliberately cantering 'on the wrong leg' is called counter canter. It requires good control and balance.**

The author's horse Quarryman in extended trot.

**Free walk on a long rein – the horse stretches his head and neck down and walks freely and purposefully forward.**

**Collected trot (above) and extended trot (below) – notice the difference in the outline and the length and shape of the strides.**

Learning to ride straight is very important. *Left* the horse is crooked and above the bit. He also has his mouth open. *Above* the rider is leaning to the right and has her left leg stuck out. The horse's head is also to the right. *Right*, here they are much straighter but still not perfect!

**Shoulder-in right.**

**Travers (haunches-in) to the left.**

**Half-pass left.**

**Emile Faurie on Virtu representing Great Britain at the Barcelona Olympics.**

**Correct salute for a dressage test.**

*Above* Carl Hester on Giorgione at the Barcelona Olympics demonstrating an expressive canter.

*Left above* Horse and rider correctly turned out for a Medium dressage test.

*Left* The author's trainer Sarah Whitmore on Dutchman in extended trot. Sarah represented Great Britain on many occasions, including the Montreal Olympics.

**The author on Quarryman in passage.**

One diagonal pair of legs no longer move together because the forehand is moving on one diagonal and the hind quarters on the other. This incorrect canter is 'disunited' – all rhythm and balance are lost and both rider and horse are very uncomfortable.

There is also a possibility that the horse loses his true canter sequence, with the canter becoming four-time instead of three-time. A four-time canter is as incorrect as a 'pacing' walk (see p.27). The cause is usually that the horse is lazy with his hind legs and the rider tries to hold the canter together with his reins. The hind leg that should work with the opposite foreleg as one beat becomes idle, taking a shorter step and touching the ground before the opposite foreleg – this makes an extra beat in the canter stride. It should not be confused with what appears to be a four-beat canter but is, in fact, in the correct sequence but missing the moment of suspension; watch the diagonal pair of legs carefully to see if they are moving together or not.

## Types of canter

There are four types of canter – working, medium, collected and extended.

The *working* canter is the basic canter. The rhythm should be clearly three-beat, with a moment of suspension after the third beat. The canter on a hard surface should be heard as a regular, clear 123.123.123. In working canter the horse must neither hurry nor labour. The speed should be such that he is well balanced, and the hind legs should be active enough to give the canter some 'lift'. In Novice dressage you are sometimes asked to show lengthened strides in canter, down the long side or on the diagonal. The judge will hope to see that the horse can lengthen his frame and therefore cover more ground with each of his strides, without quickening the rhythm or losing his balance.

The *medium* canter is much the same as lengthened strides except that a clear transition into medium is required, the strides must be sustained for a longer period and a clear transition back to working canter must be shown; therefore a greater degree of balance is required. The horse will have to engage his hocks more than in working canter. This enables him to make crisp transitions into and back from medium without falling on to his forehand and losing the quality of the canter.

The *collected* canter covers less ground than the working canter strides, but the horse bends his hocks more, creating lift and 'upwards energy', rather than 'forwards energy'. This increased engagement of the hind-quarters brings the horse's centre of gravity further back. His quarters should now appear lower than his withers and forehand, making him lighter on his feet and giving him greater freedom of the shoulders. The strides are rounder and more elevated and the neck is raised and arched. From collected canter, flying changes can be taught – this is when the horse changes from one canter lead to the other in the moment of suspension.

The *extended* canter strides should cover as much ground as possible, still in the same rhythm as collected canter. In this case, however, the energy created from behind, is used to propel the horse forwards rather than upwards. The frame of the horse should lengthen, but he must stay very well-balanced and remain totally obedient to the rider's aids, being able to return to collected canter in two or three strides – at the most!

*Strides in collected canter.*

*Strides in working canter.*

*Strides in medium canter.*

*The shape of the canter strides varies through collected, working, medium and extended, similar to that in trot.*

*Strides in extended canter.*

# CHAPTER 5

# GOING 'ON THE BIT'

'On the bit' does *not* mean that the horse has his head pulled down and his nose pulled in so that it is on the vertical line from the forehead downwards. Although faintly resembling a round outline, this artificial head position is almost certainly accompanied by an unyielding rein contact and much tension in the horse's back, and is totally incorrect.

## ROUNDNESS

The expression 'on the bit' describes a horse that is moving actively forwards from behind, into an even, elastic rein contact, in a round 'outline'. The outline is the shape in which the horse is carrying himself. A round outline is one where his neck is arched along the top line from withers to poll, with the poll as the highest point of the neck. The poll is flexed so that his nose is just in front of the vertical line which drops from his forehead. This outline will only be correct if it has been created by your legs actively pushing him forwards into the contact. If no leg has been used, his neck will be straight as opposed to arched.

**A round outline – the horse is happily 'on the bit'.**

# HOLLOWING

The opposite of a round outline is a hollow one. 'Hollow' literally describes the shape of the top line of the horse's neck. You will also find that his nose is poked out well in front of the vertical and his back is hollow and stiff.

# CONTACT

The contact is the link between your hands and the horse's mouth, through the reins. This contact enables you to give rein aids and therefore to control your horse. Riding with no contact would be similar to owning a telephone without it being connected to the network, even for 999 calls.

Control is an essential part of riding. If you encountered something frightening or dangerous while hacking, causing your horse to turn and bolt for home, how would you stop if he was not accustomed to rein aids? How would you steer him away from danger if you could not use the reins? Your horse must learn at an early age to accept a contact and to respond confidently to your rein aids.

The contact is created from the horse going *forwards* into the bridle, from your legs. This means that you must build up a connection between your legs and hands. When you use your legs you should be able to feel

that the contact becomes more secure. To maintain a steady rein contact you must maintain a steady leg contact; to increase the rein contact you must apply your legs more strongly.

Every horse is different, which means there are no hard-and-fast rules on achieving a contact. Nevertheless in one way or another every horse must go forwards from the leg into the contact.

A lazy horse first has to learn to move forwards from your leg at all costs; then he must be taught to take a light contact on the reins as he moves forwards.

A horse who runs away from the leg all the time needs to be slowed down to a speed at which you can *use* your leg to create a contact. The slowing down has to be repeated until he understands that the leg is not asking him to go faster, but to go forwards into a contact, at a steady speed.

---

## Chomping on the bit

When a horse starts to accept the contact he may chomp on the bit. This is a good sign and should not be confused with teeth-grinding, which is a resistance. Chomping on the bit produces a wet foamy mouth, which is also a good sign. A dry mouth usually indicates that the horse is fixing his jaw still to avoid an elastic contact.

---

**Left, above: A hollow outline.**

**Left, below: The horse is 'poking his nose' too much forwards. His outline needs to be rounder, although he is not as hollow as the horse in the previous picture.**

It is vital that from the beginning you offer the horse an acceptable rein contact to go forwards into. You should always aim for a light and elastic contact, with equal weight in each rein.

# EVADING THE CONTACT

If the horse does not like the contact he is being offered there are many ways he can resist it.

♂ By opening his mouth and/or drawing his tongue up or even over the bit, or by hanging his tongue out of his mouth.

♂ By fighting against the contact with his strength – twisting or raising his head or leaning on the bit.

♂ By dropping the bit. This is when he refuses to take any contact at all either by raising and shortening the neck back towards the rider or by overbending at the poll and ducking back behind the vertical.

Whichever way the horse is trying to avoid the light, elastic contact that you are seeking, it is important that you try to keep a 'feel' on the reins. Do not give with the reins every time that he drops the bit, or he will soon learn that he can avoid the contact by shortening his neck. If you can keep a feel on the reins even if his neck has shortened a great deal, he will soon learn that it is more comfortable to go with a longer neck and to accept the contact.

Likewise, the horse who leans heavily on the bit must not be allowed to continue to drag your arms from their sockets. You must regulate the contact by lightening and then checking with the rein until an acceptable contact is achieved. It is really up to you to teach the horse what contact is acceptable and what is not.

Many horses prefer to take more contact on one rein than on the other; most have a stiffer side and will try to take a heavier contact on that side. To correct this unequal contact, you must keep feeling the lighter rein to encourage the horse to connect with you, while on the heavier side you should try to lighten the contact.

Even when horse and rider have established a good contact, there will still be moments when the horse suddenly moves his head and alters the contact to an unacceptable one. When this happens the rider must first respond with the leg rather than the hand – to push the horse forward to the contact again rather than drawing him back into the contact with the hands. It is very important to remember that the contact is created from the horse going *forwards* into the bridle.

## USING THE CONTACT TO ACHIEVE ROUNDNESS

Once a contact has been achieved, you will be able to use it to develop a rounder outline. Travelling in a straight line, you can do this by pushing your horse forward with your legs and increasing the contact until he starts to yield to you and to round his neck; then you must immediately

**Right, above: An uncomfortable moment for horse and rider – the horse has come above the bit and is not accepting the contact.**

**Right, below: Here the horse is too short in the neck, and overbent – his nose is behind the vertical.**

allow with your hands (ease the
pressure) to reward him. The allowing
should not be a complete drop of the
contact but a lightening and softening
– from your elbows. It is important to
keep the pressure on the reins until
you feel the horse starting to give to
you. If you were to lighten the contact
before that, he would not understand
what you are aiming for.

Once the horse has given, and you
have relaxed your aids, he may well
bring his head up too high or off the
bit again, in which case you will have
to repeat the exercise until he learns
that you will persist until he stays
round on his own.

Never force the horse to stay on the
bit by fixing your hands and holding
his head down. You must make it
comfortable for him to be on the bit
and uncomfortable for him not to be.
If you are consistent with this, he will
very soon learn to come on to the bit
as soon as you use your legs – often
before you have used the reins.

I find that this work is best carried
out on a large circle. You can push the
horse forwards with your inside leg
into the outside-rein contact, and use
this one rein to make him rounder.
The opposite rein and leg maintain a
steady but passive contact. This can
produce a better result than using
both legs into both reins, especially
when the horse tends to have a strong
side and a soft side. If you work with
the harder rein on the inside of your
circle and the softer one on the
outside, you will be able to achieve a
firmer contact on the soft rein and
keep a lighter, more passive contact
on the hard rein. Although you
should try to work the horse on circles
to left and right, it is easier to start

with the soft rein as the outside rein.
Change direction when you have a
more equal contact and a rounder
outline.

This 'connection' between the
inside leg and the outside rein is very
important to establish; it is invaluable
in schooling all the way up to
Advanced level. The outside rein is
the main controlling rein: it regulates
the speed and controls the
straightness and bend. Over-use of
the inside rein will bring the horse's
head and neck too much to the inside.
He can then escape through his
outside shoulder and lose his
straightness.

The outside rein should not,
however, be used so strongly that the
horse actually bends his neck to the
outside. If he goes forward from your
inside leg into a good outside rein
contact, he should stretch the outside
side of his neck forwards to take a
contact on that side, rather than you
having to shorten the rein and pull his
neck to the outside to get a contact.

## LATERAL FLEXION

A good inside leg/outside rein contact
is also the basis for lateral flexion, or
bend. When the horse takes a contact
and goes on the bit, he can then be
flexed laterally in his poll. The flexion
should be to the inside on circles,
turns and in corners.

It is achieved by using your inside
leg and inside rein, supported by your
outside rein – until you can see the
horse's eye on that side. The flexion
should not be so great that the horse's
neck is turned inwards with his
shoulder drifting outwards, as this will
make him crooked.

## USING THE REINS

A soft elastic contact always comes from your *elbow*, and it is by moving your elbow that you make the rein aids. Open, flapping fingers do not create a soft contact, nor do flexible wrists – they will break the straight line that should be kept at all times between your elbow and the horse's mouth, via the reins.

The reins should be held short enough for contact to be maintained wherever the horse puts his head, while you keep the essential straight line from elbow to bit, with your elbows a little in front of your body. If your reins are too long, your elbows will be behind your body, which will make your shoulders tense. If your reins are too short, your elbows will become too straight. In both cases you will lose the elasticity that comes from having your body balanced, and your shoulders, arms and elbows in a naturally comfortable position.

If you need to shorten your reins, hold them in one hand while you slide the other hand down the reins to the desired length. Now hold the reins with this hand while you bring the first hand down to the same length. It is very important to practise this so that you maintain the contact and keep your fingers closed around the reins at all times.

The incorrect way, all too frequently seen, is to open both hands and 'walk' your fingers down the reins. This does not enable you to keep a steady contact. Worse than that, you are creating a moment when both hands are open, with fingers flapping. If your horse chose this time to shy and run away or to trip, he

*Reins held at the correct length.*

*Reins too short – the rider's arms are straight.*

*Reins too long – the rider's elbows are behind her body.*

41

would be able to pull the reins straight through your fingers and you would have lost control.

## HEAD CARRIAGE IN RELATION TO BALANCE

The position of the horse's head has a lot to do with his balance. If he carries his head very low, he is likely to be carrying too much weight on his forehand, making him unbalanced. He may lean heavily on the contact to balance himself.

To correct this, try raising your hands up and forwards for one stride and use your legs sharply to push him up to your hand. This action will indicate to him to raise his head. On no account try to pull his head up with your hands alone – this only shortens and tightens his neck, making it *more difficult* for him to come up. As you use your legs and raise your hands, lighten the contact so that he does not take the opportunity to support himself on the reins, rather than carry himself. It is your legs which must initiate the raising of the head and neck, not your hands.

Horses that tend to go too low have to be kept especially sharp to the leg. They must stay 'in front of the leg' and be pushed up into the bridle at all times. Keeping a steady rein contact is also important. This regulates the energy created by the leg aids and prevents it from pushing the horse out of balance. A low head carriage can be caused by a rider who leans forward and looks down; this is as good as an invitation to the horse to do the same.

You may have seen experienced riders working their horses very 'deep'

– that is, with the head very low but the neck still arched. Such a rider keeps his horse in balance by generating a lot of activity from behind which prevents the horse from falling on to his forehand. This is a useful exercise to stretch the muscles along the 'top-line' of the horse, making him looser in his back. This should not, however, be copied in the early stages of your training. You need to be quick to recognize and be able to correct the slightest loss of balance, otherwise you will do more harm than good.

A horse whose head carriage is too high is very often a pleasanter ride (unless his ears are in your face!) than one who is constantly trying to drag you down. It is not correct for him to raise his head and neck by hollowing his back, however. He has to carry his neck without stiffening any part of himself.

A high head carriage is often due to excitement and nerves. It is natural for the horse to raise his head when excited – watch how he reacts when he is loose in a field and something startles him. When he is tense and excited like this it will not be easy for you to get him on the bit, without first quietening him. Remember that he has to trust you. Don't try to fight him to bring his head down – he is stronger than you. Attract his attention first by walking on a circle and making simple transitions between walk and halt. Make sure you use your legs to make him walk on – don't just let him rush forwards with no aids from you.

When he starts to listen to you, rather than looking for outside interest, you will be able to start thinking about pushing him into a steady rein contact and using this rein contact to make him rounder. Stay on the circle then start to ride him from the inside leg into the outside rein contact.

When you feel that he is starting to take more contact in the outside rein, then you can resist with this rein for a moment. He should lighten to it, relax in his poll and drop down into a rounder outline. As soon as he has given you his neck like this, you must relax your aids and allow with the outside rein.

When the horse takes a good contact, keeps a round outline throughout all of his work and responds to the rein aids without altering his outline, he is truly 'on the bit' and 'accepting the bridle'.

CHAPTER 6

# RIDING TRANSITIONS, HALT AND REIN-BACK

Transitions are changes of pace – for example, between halt and walk, and between canter and trot; and, later, between collected, working, medium and extended paces. Work on transitions develops obedience and understanding and eventually helps to improve balance, so it is important to do plenty of this in your schooling.

Start by making transitions progressive, especially if they change through two paces rather than one. For instance, when halting from trot allow a few strides of walk, so that the horse does not lose his balance. When he is able to keep his balance easily and is quick to respond to your aids, you can make crisper transitions. As training progresses, you can expect increasingly good transitions.

## THE HALF-HALT IN TRANSITIONS

The half-halt is a very important part of training. As well as being used to rebalance the horse (see Chaper 7), it is used in preparation for any movement that you are about to ride, including transitions. It makes the horse more attentive to you, and more respectful of your aids. He is therefore

better able to perform whatever is required of him next.

The half-halt is exactly what it sounds like: halfway to halt and then forwards again. At first the aids may have to be repeated several times, but as training progresses the horse should become increasingly responsive to your aids – which, in turn, should become progressively light.

Before he is taught the half-halt, your horse should be able to make the simple transitions between halt, walk and trot. When he fully understands the aids for these transitions, try going from trot to walk and immediately into trot again. Repeat this, reducing the time spent in walk until it is only a fraction of a stride. These two transitions have now been amalgamated to take the form of a brief 'check' that lasts only one stride. This is a half-halt and can be ridden in all three paces.

## HOW TO RIDE TRANSITIONS

The horse must stay well-balanced, forward-going and on the bit. You should give simple, precise aids and move in balance with him into the

44

new pace. If you lose your balance, you cannot expect your horse to remain balanced or be obedient.

All transitions involve good co-ordination of your seat, leg and hand working together. There are three basic ways to use your leg:

1  A lively, 'asking' leg to move forwards to a faster pace.
2  A closing restraining leg to slow down or stop.
3  A passive 'breathing' leg to maintain the pace, ready to ask more actively when necessary.

The reins can also be used in three ways:

1  A restraining rein to slow down or stop.
2  An allowing rein to reward a reaction obtained from (1). This is a momentary lightening of the contact and should not involve a total loss of contact or make a loop in the reins.
3  A passive rein to maintain the contact created by the forward movement of the horse from your leg aids.

Use your seat in the same way:

1  Actively, by sitting heavier or lighter according to which pace you wish to increase to.
2  To restrain and slow the pace by keeping still and not moving with the horse.
3  Passively, by following the movement of the horse to maintain the current pace.

When you give the aids for a transition, you must allow your body to go with the horse into the pace you have asked for. It is no good asking him to move forwards from walk into trot if you sit rigid and unyielding like a rock in the saddle. Even though your legs may have asked him to trot, the rest of your body is telling him not to move.

To understand how to follow the movement of the horse with your body, remember how he moves in his three basic paces. In the walk he moves his four legs independently but in a regular sequence and rhythm. There is no suspension in the walk but there should be a supple swing through his body as he moves. Do not try to exaggerate this swing by rocking your hips from side to side. Just allow him to carry you forwards, keeping your back firm and supportive, your hips relaxed and your seat comfortably on the saddle. There should be no up-and-down movement that throws you out of the saddle at all. Let your elbows move forwards with the contact and allow them to follow the movement of the horse's head and neck.

## Halt to walk

To proceed in walk from halt, keep your seat and upper body still and relaxed, then ask lightly with both legs until you feel the horse start to move. Stop asking at that point but leave your legs close to his sides. Without gripping, let them move against him in the rhythm of the walk. If the walk is lazy and lifeless, use a quick, light kick to liven him. If he does not respond, use the leg a bit harder or touch him with your whip, then immediately relax to check that he is now going forwards for himself. On no account should you 'squeeze' your legs tightly around him; closing your leg will be the aid for him to halt.

## Walk to trot

The trot is a more lively pace than the walk, with two beats to each stride and a moment of suspension between each beat. You should sit lightly in trot and allow the horse to push you upwards. If you sit too heavily he will not be able to carry you easily; his trot will lose its spring or he may even break into a canter. Your legs should stay close to his sides, but should not be tight in any way.

The aids to maintain the trot are simply to go with him in a relaxed but balanced way and to use your legs lightly whenever necessary – this should not be a continuous drumming every stride or his sides will become numb. Remember to change your diagonal often to keep him from getting one-sided (see p.28).

To ride forwards from walk to trot, prepare the horse with a half-halt. This tells him that something is going to happen. Then, sitting lightly but still, ask him to move forwards into trot with quicker, more energetic leg aids than for walk. Try to give two or three little aids in the rhythm that you want in the trot. As soon as you feel the first step of trot, make sure that you are sitting lightly and in balance. If you sit too heavily, he may stiffen his back against your weight and run into a flat trot or even canter. If you are going to do rising trot, it is usually a good idea to sit for the first couple of strides, until the trot is established, then start to rise, on the correct diagonal. The point of sitting is to enable the horse to find his balance

and rhythm before you start moving your body around. If, however, the horse has a 'cold' back, feels as if he might buck or is very tense and excited, you should start rising at once.

A 'cold'-backed horse is one that feels uncomfortable when the saddle is first on, resenting the girth being tightened and humping his back against the weight of the rider. This could be due to a back problem (which you should get the vet to check) or to a bad experience in the past. It is sensible with a horse like this to put the saddle on about 20 minutes before you mount. Use a well-padded numnah and make sure that it and the girth are kept clean and dry. Tighten the girth very gradually. Fill in the time before you start with odd jobs around the yard, so that you are near the horse without actually fussing over him. Get on from a mounting block and lower yourself quietly into the saddle. Do *not* land with a bump – on *any* horse.

## Trot to walk

To make a transition from trot to walk, first half-halt to make sure you have the horse's attention. Then *close* your lower legs, just behind the girth. instead of keeping them relaxed and 'breathing' as you would to maintain the trot. Sit still and restrain a little with your reins. As he begins to walk, immediately allow with the reins, relax your legs into the passive position and ride him forwards in the walk.

## Trot to halt

To halt from trot, the aids are similar to those for walk, but your legs should remain firmly closed around the horse until he has stopped. They should stay closed in the halt itself so that he maintains a contact on the bit. Restrain with the reins until he has halted then immediately allow – enough to reward him for stopping, but not so much that he walks on again or thinks he can have a rest and stretch his neck.

## Halt to trot

If a light leg and rein contact are maintained in the halt, the horse will remain 'on the aids' and it will be easy to proceed into trot again by using both legs energetically in the trot rhythm, keeping a passive contact on the reins and letting your body go forwards with him.

## Trot to canter

The transition from trot to canter, also called the 'strike off', needs careful preparation to make sure that you obtain the correct canter lead. It is easier to do this in a corner than on a straight line. If you do get an incorrect strike off, come back to trot and prepare to try again in the next corner.

To prepare for a strike off, make sure that the horse is sharp to your aids and steady on the bit, and that he has enough impulsion to propel him into canter; a laboured trot will probably not give him enough lift to get into canter. You need a little bend to the inside, but he must not be crooked either before or after the strike off.

Approaching the corner, make a half-halt. As the horse comes back to you, sit down firmly in the saddle with a fraction more weight on your inside seatbone, bring your outside leg back behind the girth and press firmly with

your inside leg on the girth. Keep a steady contact on the outside rein and lighten the inside rein.

You should now be in canter. If you are not, quickly half-halt again and repeat the aids as clearly as you can. Tap him with the whip if necessary. Be ready to half-halt and repeat again if he runs faster in trot instead of cantering. Use the whip just behind your *inside* leg if possible, as this is the leg that initiates the canter.

To maintain the canter, your inside leg must stay on the girth and can be used on the first beat of the stride to create more activity. Your seat should be still in the saddle following the horse's body movement – down, forwards, up – on each stride. Do not try to exaggerate this by rocking your upper body backwards and forwards but do try to go with him. Your outside leg should stay passive behind the girth, to keep the quarters from falling out. It may need to be used occasionally with the inside leg if the horse is lazy and needs a good thump to go forwards.

## Canter to trot

To return to trot from canter, sit still (instead of following the movement of the horse) and close your legs just behind the girth. You may need to resist a little with the hand as well but only momentarily; too much use of the reins in any transition is likely to restrict the horse's head and neck movement. This will cause him to fall onto his forehand and to lean on the reins. As soon as you are in trot, resume your aids for 'maintaining the trot' as explained in 'walk to trot'.

After a short canter, the horse will often offer you more energy in his trot.

Do not allow him to turn this into excess speed, but try to use it to create more impulsion and perhaps to develop lengthened strides and medium trot (see p. 30).

## Change of lead through trot

When your transitions between trot and canter are well-established, you can try changing from one canter lead to the other, with approximately three strides of trot in between. This is not an exercise to see how quickly you can change legs by hurling the horse from one rein on to the other with minimum strides in trot, but it *is* a test of obedience, balance and straightness.

The transition from canter to trot must be crisp, with the horse maintaining balance and impulsion to carry him forwards into several free, regular trot strides. You must be able to change the bend, make a half-halt and give the aids for the new canter, all within a couple of strides.

The trot strides are just as important as the canter and the transition. If the trot is hurried and unbalanced, it is better to stay in trot for long enough to rebalance the horse before cantering again – a poor trot will result in a muddled transition to canter.

This exercise can be performed on a straight line across the diagonal or between two half-circles.

## Walk to canter

When the horse is well-balanced enough to canter slowly and can shorten his stride within the same rhythm, you can start to work towards transitions to walk and directly from walk to canter. The

latter is the easier of the two, but it does require the horse to be very sharp to your leg aids and to be active in walk.

To prepare for canter from walk, improve the activity in the walk through several half-halts. Then sit down more on your seat bones, especially the inside one, press the inside leg on to the girth and let the outside leg come behind the girth, to prevent the horse swinging to the outside.

By now you should understand clearly the difference in your aids between those for trot and those for canter from the walk. For trot the seat is light and allowing, the legs are light and energetic and moving as a pair. For canter the seat is firmer in the saddle, and the legs are moving independently of each other; the aid, which is slower and stronger, is coming from the inside leg only, but is supported by the outside leg.

## Canter to walk

To prepare the canter for a downwards transition to walk, you must be able to achieve and maintain a degree of collection. Although it is quite possible to make the downward transition by leaning back and throwing your whole weight back against the reins, this is incorrect. It should only be used as an 'emergency stop' when in danger.

The correct approach is to collect the canter through half-halts, so that the horse gradually carries more weight on his hind legs and engages them further under his body. You must be able to slow the speed of the canter almost to that of the walk within a couple of strides and then to ride forwards in the canter again.

The horse should not be asked to shorten his stride and collect for too long at a time because it is very hard work for him. If his muscles start to ache he may look for a way to avoid doing what you ask. The same applies to any work that is new or more difficult – you must be satisfied with short spells of good progress and then return to easier work. A generous horse can quickly become sour and unwilling if his efforts are not rewarded by praise and a short rest.

When you are able to collect the canter for a few strides, it is quite easy to drop into walk by sitting down, closing the lower legs and restraining for a moment with the reins. Always push the horse forwards into a good walk; do not collapse after the transition and let him stop dead.

### Simple change through walk

A simple change through walk is the next exercise you can do to master these transitions. The exercise is similar to the change of lead through trot; about three clear strides of good-quality walk should be shown. The walk is very important. If the horse starts to anticipate the canter he must be made to stay in walk (walking a small circle will soon get him under control again) until the walk steps are good.

### Counter canter

There are no specific transitions into and out of counter canter (cantering with the outside leg leading). You do, however, need to know how to maintain the original canter lead when you go from true canter to counter canter. By sitting correctly you will help the horse to maintain his balance and the correct lead.

For now, assume that you are cantering on the left lead. As you begin the counter canter, you should keep a little more weight on your left seat bone, so that you are sitting above the leading leg. Your left leg should stay forwards on the girth to maintain the impulsion – it must not become tense and must not move back because this might initiate a flying change. Your right leg should stay a little behind the girth but should not be too strong or the quarters will swing to the left.

Keep a slight flexion (bend) to the left, and keep your body pointing in the direction in which the horse is going – more to the right than for true canter – with your shoulders and hips parallel with the horse's shoulders and hips. If the counter canter is on a curve to the right, your right shoulder will be further back than your left, and also your hip, but without twisting or stiffening your body.

## THE HALT

The halt sounds simple, but making a correct halt takes concentration and control. The difference between halting and just stopping is that in the halt the horse must be alert and well-balanced enough to be able to move off in any pace, whereas 'stopping' is just standing still. The horse should learn in the very first stages of his training to stand still, without fidgeting.

Do not fiddle about trying to make him square too early on; wait until he can keep his balance coming in to the halt. Keep your legs closed around the

A good halt (*opposite, above*). The horse is standing with his hocks well underneath him in a good outline. He is quiet, immobile and so 'square' that only two legs can be seen from the side. (*Above*) The same halt, from behind. Notice how straight horse and rider are.

A poor halt (*opposite, above*). The horse appears unsettled – he is not standing square or balanced, and he is above the bit.

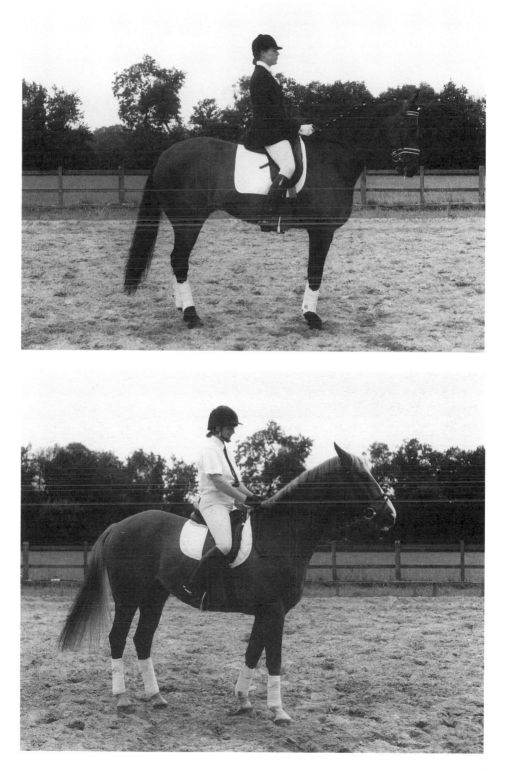

**When the horse has halted well, he should remain still and quiet; here the rider has rewarded him with a long rein.**

horse to keep him steady on the bit, and maintain a light rein contact. Always reward him with a pat when he has halted well.

## REIN-BACK

The rein-back is a backwards stepping movement in two-time. The horse moves his legs in diagonal pairs, as in trot, but there is no moment of suspension. He should pick his feet up well and not drag them.

The rein-back is quite demanding on the horse's back muscles so it should not be repeated too many times. He should always be ridden forwards immediately after going back – never halt after going back.

If your horse is well-handled in the stable you have probably taught him to move back by standing in front of him, giving him a nudge on the chest with your fist and saying 'back' until he responds, then releasing your aids and praising him. If you have someone

## The rein-back.

to help you, it will be very simple to teach him the aids from the rider by using them in conjunction with the aids that he already understands from the person on the ground. As he starts to understand your aids from the saddle, the person on the ground can do less and less, and finally move away.

Before you ask for a rein-back the horse must be well-balanced in a good halt. To start the rein-back, bring your upper body forwards just enough to lighten your seat. Taking your weight off his back makes it easier for him to move back while he is learning; once he is established in the movement this will not be necessary. Your legs should remain passive but close enough to his sides to straighten him if he starts to go crooked.

Restrain him from moving forwards with your reins, increase the contact for a moment and as soon as you feel that he starts to move even a tiny bit back reward him by allowing with the hand. In the next second restrain with your reins again to ask for another step back. You must always allow immediately that he starts to go back and then increase the contact again for the next step.

At first, be satisfied with one or two steps back, then walk forwards and praise the horse. When that comes easily then you can ask for three or four steps back. This is adequate for dressage tests up to Medium level. At Advanced level, five or six steps are required but horses have developed greater strength in their backs by this stage and will not find it difficult.

# CHAPTER 7

# DEVELOPING RHYTHM, BALANCE AND IMPULSION

When a horse is well-balanced throughout all of his work, being able to maintain this total balance or self-carriage, in corners, transitions and movements, he will earn good marks in a dressage test and will be able to progress to a high level. In its simplest form, balance is having the correct amount of speed and impulsion (controlled energy), achieved through effective use of half-halts.

Remember that when you sit on a horse, you bring his centre of gravity further forwards, putting him 'on the forehand' and upsetting his balance. In this chapter we are going to look at how you can bring him back into balance through half-halts, so that his centre of gravity comes back, his hind legs start to carry more weight, and he is then able to carry himself *and you*.

## RHYTHM AND BALANCE

Rhythm and balance go more or less hand in hand. A horse is not able to stay in balance unless he can keep a steady rhythm in each of his paces; in the same way his rhythm will be lost if he loses his balance.

To develop a steady rhythm in each pace, it often helps to count aloud the beats of each stride. There should be a little gap for the moment of suspension in trot: 1.2.1.2.1.2. The tempo, or speed of the rhythm, is important too – if the trot is too hurried and there is no moment of suspension then it would be: 121212. The canter should be 123.123.123. allowing for the short moment of suspension in each stride; again, if the tempo is too hurried it will be 123123123. Because the walk has no moment of suspension it will be 123412341234, but if very hurried it may become an incorrect two-beat pace. If you cannot feel the beats of each stride clearly in any of the paces, slow down to give yourself more time to feel how your horse is moving.

The best speed is that which allows you to develop a good rhythm. The horse's speed should be such that he moves actively and freely forwards, keeping an even rhythm but not

**Right, above: A well-balanced canter. The horse appears to be going 'uphill'.**

**Right, below: A poorly balanced trot. The horse is on the forehand and opening his mouth in resistance.**

hurrying. The speed is too fast if he takes uneven strides and tends to quicken through corners, and too slow if he labours through the corners, almost falling into walk.

Once you can feel the movement of each stride you will begin to recognize when they are regular and rhythmical. To keep good rhythm, every stride must be exactly the same length. Each stride must also be the same height off the ground and must take the same time before it touches the ground again.

---

### Like clockwork

If you find it difficult to judge when the rhythm is regular, it can be helpful to use a metronome, a clockwork device that 'ticks' rhythmically at any speed you set it. It is used by musicians to help them keep time. It will help you to keep the same rhythm and speed in the corners and on turns and circles as you do on straight lines. You will need someone to help you set the metronome to the right speed for each pace; a quartz metronome is best as you can carry it in your pocket and it will work even when it is bumping around upside down.

---

Some horses have natural rhythm, and are able to keep it when ridden. This is an advantage in a dressage horse provided that the stride is flexible enough to lengthen and shorten.

Some horses show good rhythm on the lunge or when loose but lose it when ridden. They need to re-establish their rhythm in order to regain their balance while carrying the rider.

Others appear to have little or no rhythm. This is often due to being ridden at the wrong speed, leading to loss of balance. When a horse is like this, it is possible eventually to develop rhythm, provided that you have a feel for rhythm yourself and are patient enough to keep correcting it.

## IMPULSION

Being able to regulate the speed, rhythm and tempo is the first priority but it is not the only factor keeping the horse in balance. Impulsion, which can be described as controlled energy, is the other factor. It is an essential part of the horse's way of going, it gives lightness and elasticity to his paces. To create impulsion, you have to regulate and direct the energy and the desire to move forwards that your horse offers you. If he offers you no energy or desire to move forwards, you will first have to achieve this by improving his reaction to your leg and by sharpening him up. If he is allowed to use his energy and power against his rider, a horse can become unmanageable, but if he is taught at an early age to be obedient, his energy can be directed into impulsion.

Impulsion starts with the ability to transfer more weight on to the hind quarters. This brings the centre of gravity back, which is to the rider's advantage.

The horse should bend the three joints in his hind legs – the hip, stifle, and hock joint – equally. The hind legs need to create greater activity in order to step further under his body and carry a greater proportion of his weight. His back should be supple, to allow the energy created by his hind

*Centre of gravity forwards – this horse is poorly balanced and will not be able to develop impulsion whilst he is bearing down onto his forehand.*

*Centre of gravity further back – this horse appears to be going 'uphill' in a good balance.*

legs to swing forwards through his whole body giving him an overall appearance of lightness, springiness and elasticity in his movement.

When the horse moves in balance, with good impulsion, he appears to move upwards and forwards at the withers, with freedom in his shoulders and bending of his knees. His neck is raised and arched, with the poll as the highest point. The nose is a fraction in front of the vertical line down from his forehead, and his jaw is relaxed, quietly accepting the contact.

To be able to build up impulsion, you must be in control of the speed and tempo. You must be able to 'drive' the horse without him running away. Likewise, the horse must *want* to go forwards and must be 'on the aids' and 'on the bit' (see Chapter 5). Work on transitions and half-halts (see Chapter 6) is an excellent way to build up impulsion without losing control.

## USE OF THE HALF-HALT IN REBALANCING

The aids that the horse first learned taught him to go forwards from the leg. Now he must learn that the leg does not always mean 'go faster' it also means 'go at the same speed with more energy'. This is where the half-halt becomes very important. Chapter 6 explained the importance of the half-halt in relation to transitions; now you will learn how it can be used to improve balance and develop impulsion.

You will remember that the half-halt is a check that brings the horse halfway to halt and then forward again. It is therefore a useful way of getting his attention and ensuring

that he is obedient, but it also enables you to reduce speed and regenerate impulsion.

In a half-halt the momentary reduction in speed allows the horse's hind legs to step further under his body. If you can instantly make use of this increased engagement of his hind legs to make them more active, they will be able to carry a greater proportion of his weight – and this improves his balance.

The success of each half-halt depends on the horse's obedience and his acceptance of your aids. If your horse rushes forward every time you use your leg, you will have to spend time patiently correcting him and repeating the half-halt until he understands.

Even with a more advanced horse there are times when he will forget himself and run forward from the leg. You must quietly slow him down then ask him again with your leg very lightly. If he runs forward again do not worry; just continue repeating it until his response becomes better. If you are patient, if your aids are clear and if you are quick to praise when there is an improvement, then he will learn quickly.

If you have difficulty with half-halts, it may be because you have not fully established a correct seat and good balance. This would prevent you from giving aids that are clear enough for him to react to in the desired way. The result – both horse and rider end up confused. I stress again the vital importance of learning how to sit correctly and effectively so that you keep your balance at all times and are able to give good aids.

As soon as you have taught your

horse to half-halt, you will begin to feel the benefits. It is well worth spending time to establish it at this stage if you want to improve your horse's balance and way of going, and make him a pleasanter ride. You will be able to use the half-halt not only to improve your horse's balance, by reducing speed and increasing impulsion, but also to 'set him up' for whatever you may ask him to do next.

A top rider once told me that on the journey to a very important competition, he had not passed the time by thinking through the movements of the test, as one might imagine, but by thinking through the test in terms of where he would need to make his half-halts.

The half-halt is an important way of altering the horse's balance, so that he is not 'on the forehand'. Being 'on the forehand' means the horse is unbalanced and his centre of gravity has come too far forwards, restricting the freedom of his shoulders and losing the engagement of his hind legs. He will be uncomfortable to ride and may lean on the rider's hands to support his head. Every movement will be more difficult.

The horse often gets on the forehand because his speed is too fast for the amount of impulsion. This is where the half-halt is very useful – to slow the speed and increase the impulsion.

One correction will not prevent

**Group high in canter – this young horse has lost his balance coming out of a corner.**

your horse from going on the forehand ever again; it will be a continuous process of encouraging him to take more weight on his hind legs and lighten his forehand. The important thing is to learn to feel when the horse is beginning to go on his forehand, and to be able to correct him immediately. The longer you leave it, the more difficult it is to correct.

The conformation of a horse may throw it on to the forehand. This occurs when the croup is higher than the point of the withers or the shoulders are very 'loaded' and the hind quarters lighter. In this case it is even more important that you are able to help the horse to balance himself with effective half-halts.

When the horse falls temporarily on his forehand, it may seem that he is going downhill. If he stiffens his back in the canter due to being on the forehand, his croup may come higher than his withers; this is called 'croup high'. It may not be a conformation fault but perhaps a temporary schooling problem.

A tendency to be on the forehand will usually be accentuated in the more demanding movements. For example, in lengthened strides at the trot, a horse whose hind legs are insufficiently engaged will often go 'wide behind'. This means that he compensates for the fact that he doesn't step under with his hind legs by stepping out to the side with each hind leg. He maintains activity in his hind legs but has stiffened through his back. This can also happen when the rider asks for more lengthening than the horse is capable of or when the rider sits very heavily.

## CADENCE AND SELF-CARRIAGE

When the horse maintains good rhythm, balance and impulsion, he is able to develop a quality called 'cadence'. This is an overall feeling of elasticity and softness but also of power and athleticism that can be felt and seen. Cadence does not develop in isolation. It comes as a result of extreme regularity in the rhythm, enormous impulsion and an ability to stay in balance throughout all the horse's work.

There will eventually be a time when the horse remains in balance throughout every movement with only the smallest of half-halts at intervals; this is called self-carriage. The degree of self-carriage is relative to the level the horse is working at, but as a guide the horse should not be taught any new movements until he can stay in self-carriage in all the movements he is currently doing.

**Wide behind in lengthened strides – although this horse's near hind is directly following his near fore, his off hind is to the right of his off fore.**

CHAPTER 8

# STRAIGHTNESS AND SUPPLENESS

The various factors discussed in Chapter 7 which contribute to balance and self-carriage are not complete without a reference to straightness and suppleness. These are so important that they have been given a chapter of their own.

## STRAIGHTNESS

Before you are able to ride circles and figures, you must be able to ride true straight lines. On the straight line your horse must be absolutely straight through his body. His hind legs follow his forelegs, which means that his hind feet follow the tracks of his forefeet. The value of a straight horse is that he is easier to steer and therefore more controllable. He will

develop his muscles equally on each side of his body, and so find it easier to balance himself. A straight horse will be able to develop suppleness.

Crookedness is the opposite to straightness. A crooked horse moves with his hind feet following in different tracks from the forefeet – either to the right or to the left of the corresponding front foot, or when on a curve to the inside or to the outside.

### Careless riding

Too much use of one rein or one leg or a poor position – are common causes of crookedness. A crooked rider makes a crooked horse. The degree of crookedness depends on the sensitivity of the horse and the relative size of horse and rider. A small rider on a large, wide cob will do less

*Straightness – Tracks of hindfeet following those of forefeet.*

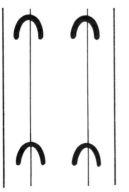

*Crookedness – Tracks of hindfeet not following those of forefeet.*

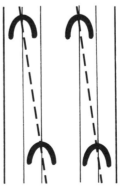

**Crookedness – the horse has his hindquarters to the left and his forehand to the right.**

damage than a large rider on a narrow, light thoroughbred.

A rider who does not sit equally on each seat bone, in the middle of the saddle, with the upper body straight and both legs positioned the same, must correct the seat and sit straight and balanced on the horse before seeking to improve the horse.

---

### Ride a crooked mile

A rider may be sitting straight, but must also *ride* the horse straight. If there is more weight in one rein than the other (which may well happen without the rider realizing it) the horse will become stronger on that side and may also start to go crooked.

---

Asking for too much bend can cause crookedness. A degree of bend can be achieved without losing straightness – this is not contradictory because straightness is not a straight line from head to tail, but occurs when the hind legs follow the forelegs. A horse cannot actually bend in his spine. He can, however, give the appearance of a uniform bend throughout his whole body, so that although the vertebrae may not move, the supporting muscles and tissues do.

It is in his neck that he can give the most bend and this is usually the cause of the crookedness. If the neck is bent too much to one side, which easily happens with some horses, the shoulder on the opposite side will start to drift away from the bend. The forelegs will follow the shoulders, and the hind legs will no longer be behind them. This exaggerated bend often

results when an inexperienced rider learns to bend the horse, without knowing quite how much bend there should be.

I always insist that a rider must ride the horse straight before asking for any bend, be able to recognize straightness and know how to achieve

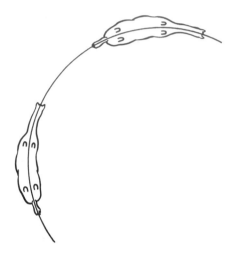

*The bend in the horse's body should match the curve that he is on.*

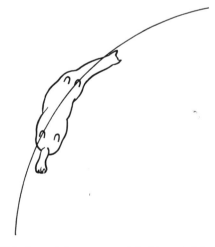

*If the horse is bent too much in his neck, his shoulder may fall to the outside, his hindfeet are no longer following the tracks of his forefeet.*

it. It will then be much easier to correct any crookedness that occurs owing to too much bend – simply by straightening the neck and forgoing the bend.

The amount of bend through the horse should match the curve he is on. On a straight line he should not bend at all, but when riding a circle he should be cut in half from head to tail by the line of the circle.

## Crookedness in the horse

Some horses are crooked without a rider, and this can be seen while trotting up in hand. The crookedness may have been caused by incorrect riding, or it may be due to a weakness somewhere in his body. If he is always crooked in the same way, it is possible that something is out of place in his back, which could also cause uneven muscle development.

If you are worried that your horse always seems to be crooked or is stiff on one side, it is a good idea to ask your vet to check his back next time you see him. If there is nothing wrong you can work the horse without the constant worry that what you are doing may be hurting him. If there is a problem, your vet may be able to sort it out himself, or he may suggest you call in someone who specializes in backs – perhaps a physiotherapist or osteopath.

Crookedness often occurs in young, unbalanced horses. The shoulders fall to the outside on turns and circles, the rider is unable to ride a straight line with the hind feet following the tracks of the forefeet. This is temporary and will improve with schooling as the horse learns to go forwards into a steady rein contact.

In a case like this the rider must be careful to keep his own balance and straightness even when the horse has lost his; once the rider has become crooked, even as a result of the horse's crookedness, it is more difficult for the horse to correct himself.

The rider should correct this crookedness in the horse by using both legs to drive him forwards into a more even rein contact and should not just use the inside leg to push the quarters out. Half-halts should be used to maintain the balance. When the horse takes an even contact on the bit and the rider sits straight, the horse's shoulders will come in on to the track and he will be straight again. Remember that a crooked horse can not be straightened until the rider's own position is right.

Chapter 7 explained how a horse can go wide behind or croup high when his hind legs are not sufficiently engaged to maintain self-carriage. He may also try to avoid engaging his hind legs by bringing them to one side rather than under his body, causing crookedness.

It often happens in canter, when the horse brings his quarters to the inside. This may be a sign that he is being asked to canter slower than he can and to engage his hind legs more than he is able to.

It must be corrected as soon as possible, either by riding the canter more forwards or by straightening as follows. Bring your hands a little to the inside, encouraging the forehand to come to the inside, while using the inside leg on the girth to keep the horse's body on the track.

While you are making this correction, make sure that you are sitting straight, not leaning to the side. Your seat bones *must* be in the middle of the saddle, with your body evenly balanced above them.

## SUPPLENESS

When a horse uses his body in an athletic way, developing power from his hind quarters, swinging through his back with freedom in his shoulders and with his neck flexible enough to bend either way if required, his paces will become springy and elastic, giving added quality to his way of going. It is this quality that we call suppleness.

A supple horse feels loose, flexible and bouncy, in a soft way, and is a much more comfortable ride.

The opposite of supple is stiff. Stiffness, which has a variety of causes, hampers the horse's progress and gives a jarring ride through tightness in the back. The paces of a stiff horse tend to be restricted.

Conformation, the way that a horse is put together, does dictate to a certain extent how he moves. However, even the most beautifully made horse may not necessarily move well. To make the very best of your horse, you must make him as supple as possible. Suppleness is an essential quality for a dressage horse. It must be developed with correct work through the whole of the horse's body – his back, limbs, neck, poll, jaw and even his mind.

### Suppling exercises

Suppling exercises are those that stretch and bend the horse, developing looseness and flexibility in the way that he moves and carries himself. Many horses have a stiff side; that is, they find it less easy to bend to that side and move less freely when on a circle in that direction. Although it helps to spend more time working in the stiffer direction – until the horse is equal on both sides – it is very important to make frequent changes of direction so that the horse does not become fixed in one position.

When you bend your horse, say, to the right, his right side is being shortened by this exercise and his left side is being stretched. Therefore, if he is stiffer to the right, it sometimes helps to go to the left so that his right side is being stretched and loosened up, rather than shortened. Many of the basic movements and figures covered in Chapter 9 are specially designed to develop suppleness.

It is always a good idea to assess your horse's good points and his bad points. Analyse what he has and does *naturally* – the more you learn about him, the better you will understand how to improve him.

CHAPTER 9

# RIDING SOME BASIC MOVEMENTS

If you have followed the previous chapters carefully, your horse should by now be obedient, well-balanced, on the bit, supple and straight. You will need to keep working at all of these to maintain and improve them throughout his training, but you should now be able to perform satisfactorily some of the movements that are required in Novice dressage tests. Although you may already have ridden some of these, this chapter should help to clarify exactly what you are aiming for in each movement.

To start with, you need to know the exact size of the area that you are working in. 20 × 20 m (22 yd × 22 yd) is the minimum required to provide

enough room to perform the movements in; 20 m × 40 m (22 yd × 44 yd) would be much better. You will need to put some markers around your area, as described on p. 18, to enable you to ride the movements accurately. Accuracy is vital: as self-discipline and a guide to how well in control you really are.

The basic figures are circles, half-circles, loops and serpentines. Look carefully at the line drawings, even drawing them out yourself on paper before you attempt to ride them, so that you see clearly where to go. Try riding them first in walk, to get the feel of the movement. Later, progress to trot and perhaps canter.

*Using a 20 × 40 metre arena showing different ways to change the rein, and how to ride the corners.*

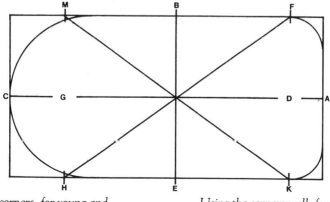

*Cutting the corners, for young and unbalanced horses this is easier.*

*Using the corners well, for more advanced horses.*

## Using a 40 × 20 metre arena

*Going 'large'*

When going 'large' (ie riding around the track) you should ride the corners as a quarter-circle rather than a right-angle turn, which would unbalance your horse; the quarter-circle should be of a size that you can ride easily. At Advanced level your corners might be equivalent to a quarter of a circle 6 m (6 yd) in diameter, but at Novice level they might be a quarter of a circle 15 m (16 yd).

*Changes of direction*

Changing direction, or 'changing the rein', can be done by turning straight across the arena from B to E, or straight down the centre line from A to C, then turning on to the other rein. These turns, like corners, should be ridden as quarter-circles of the appropriate size. You can also change the rein across the diagonal line, for example MXK, or by riding half-circles, which are covered on p. 71.

required in dressage tests becomes smaller the higher the level of test. In training, you can make smaller circles as your horse becomes better balanced and more obedient.

You should bend your horse to match the curve of the circle that he is on. For a 20 m (22 yd) circle this is very little, but for a smaller circle it will be more, so do not attempt a circle smaller than the bend he is able to manage.

Ask for the inside bend by using your inside leg on the girth and your outside rein to control the amount of bend. Indicate the bend with the inside rein but don't force the bend by pulling back, or the horse's shoulder will fall to the outside and he will become crooked and lose his balance. His shoulder could also fall to the outside if you do not have a contact on the outside rein. Too much outside rein, however, will block the inside bend, making him stiff and unable to bend at all.

*Bend the horse according to the size of the circle you are riding.*

## CIRCLES

Working on circles and half-circles helps to make the horse more supple. He has to engage his inside hind leg more underneath his body to enable him to turn continuously. With his outside hind leg he has to stretch a little more than on a straight line as the outside legs have to travel slightly further than the inside legs. Frequent changes of rein ensure that the horse is equally supple on both sides.

In general terms, the size of circles

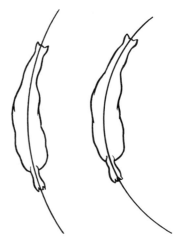

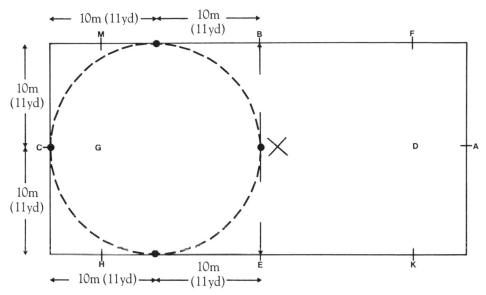

*A 20 metre circle – find the 'four points' of your circle and join them with a smooth curve.*

Circles are referred to by their diameter. The largest and therefore the simplest is the 20 m (22 yd) circle.

### 20 metre circles
A 20 m (22 yd) circle takes up the full width of a 20 m × 40 m (22 yd × 44 yd) arena and half its length. The circle should always start clearly at a marker, such as A, B or X. To find the right size and shape, you need to look at four points in the circle, then ride from point to point with a smooth curve.

Imagine starting the circle at B on the left rein. You should leave the track directly after B, and cross the centre line exactly halfway between X and C; here you should be parallel with the short side of the arena. Next touch the track just before E so that as you pass the marker you are straight on the track. In the very next stride leave the track and then cross the centre line exactly halfway between X and A, again making sure that you are straight across the arena as you cross

the centre line. Rejoin the track just before B so that as you pass B you are straight on the track. Each step of the circle should turn you a fraction of a metre so that every step is on a curve and no step is straight ahead.

In a test you make one circle at a time, but when schooling it is useful to do some of your work on a continuous 20 m (22 yd) circle, provided that you keep the shape and do not allow the horse to wander. You must pay attention to every single step, so that you follow the hoof prints of the previous round. After some time on the same circle you will start to see a clear track where you have been. You can change the rein through the middle of the circle; this is a good test of your control and steering.

If you make transitions on a circle be very careful not to drift off the circle as you change pace. The faster you go, the quicker you have to be with the steering. As you slow down, be careful not to turn too sharply – follow the curve of the circle all the time.

69

**Riding a 10 metre circle at C.**

## 15 metre circles

A 15 m (16 yd) circle requires more balance and suppleness than a 20 m (22 yd) circle. It is also more difficult for you to see how big it should be because there are no clear points to guide you.

When starting at B, the middle of the circle will be on the B to X line,

2.5 m (8 ft) from X and 7.5 m (25 ft) from B. To make the circle round you must stay 7.5 m (25 ft) from the middle of it, all the time. The circle will cross the X to E line exactly halfway between X and E.

The easiest way to see exactly where your circle will go is by drawing a scale diagram on paper.

*A 15 metre circle left, starting at B.*

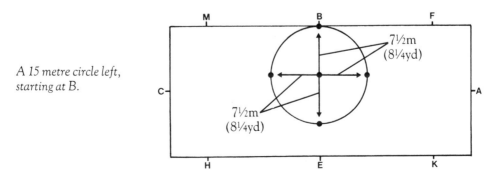

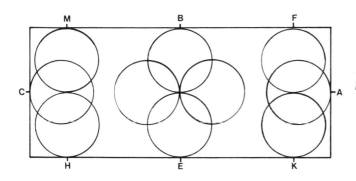

*10 metre circles can be performed at any marker.*

## 10 metre circles

A 10 m (11 yd) circle can be performed at any of the markers in a 20 m × 40 m (22 yd × 44 yd) arena. Your horse must be able to keep his balance easily on a 15 m (16 yd) circle before you try a smaller one. It is quite easy to gauge the size: 10 m (11 yd) is half the width of the arena. If you make your circle at a quarter marker (M, F, H or K), however, note that these markers are 6 m (6 yd) from the corners. Therefore, the circle does not touch the short side of the arena but comes one metre (yard) short of it.

## Smaller circles

Circles of 8 m (26 ft) and 6 m (6 yd) are sometimes required in Advanced

tests, but a high degree of collection and balance is needed for the horse to perform such small circles well.

## HALF-CIRCLES

Half-circles are useful for changing the rein, and several half-circles one after another are a good suppling exercise. A half-circle should be exactly the shape and size that half of a whole circle would be. Sometimes a half-circle can be followed by riding in a straight line, returning to the track to change the rein. Alternatively, the half-circle can be followed immediately by a half-circle on the other rein. The half-circle can be any of the sizes that your whole circles are.

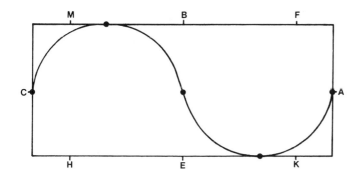

*A half-20 metre circle from A to X, followed by another from X to C.*

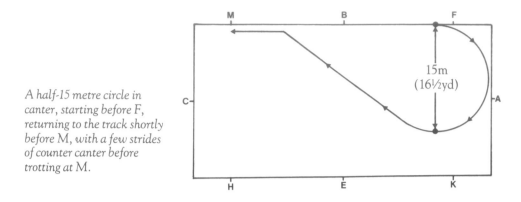

*A half-15 metre circle in canter, starting before F, returning to the track shortly before M, with a few strides of counter canter before trotting at M.*

## Half 15 metre circles

These are often done in canter, as an introduction to counter canter. They should be started on the long side of the arena, at least 1.5 m (5 ft) before the last quarter marker. This allows you 7.5 m (25 ft) clear of the short side. The widest point will be halfway between the centre line and the opposite long side.

## Half 10 metre circles

These too are useful for introducing counter canter. They are used in trot when changing the rein and also for progression towards smaller circles, when the horse is well balanced in 15 m (16 yd) and 20 m (22 yd) circles It is wise to ride half 10 m (11 yd) circles before attempting full 10 m (11 yd)

circles, thus introducing a greater degree of difficulty gradually. Two or more half circles can be ridden one after another, to improve the horse's suppleness; this requires accurate riding.

While on a 20 m circle, as recommended in the previous chapters, it is useful to be able to change the rein within the circle by making two half 10 (11 yd) circles.

## LOOPS

Suppling work similar to circles and half circles can also be done on loops. A loop is performed from the long side of the arena, as shown in the diagram, moving 3 or 5 m (10 or 16 ft) from the track at the widest point of the loop.

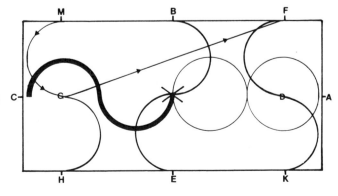

*Half-10 metre circles can be ridden at any marker in the arena and can be followed by another or by a straight line to the track.*

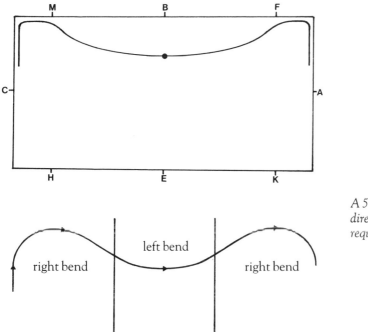

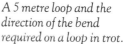

*A 5 metre loop and the direction of the bend required on a loop in trot.*

The size of the loop is measured at the point where you cross the B to E line; this is the widest point of the loop. If you ride the loop in trot, you should start with a little inside bend, and straighten out when you are on the straight line. As you turn to the outside in the middle of the loop, bend the horse to the outside. As you return to the track in a straight line, straighten him again and as you reach the track before the corner bend him to the inside.

Riding the loop in canter is altogether different. You will maintain the canter on the inside leg throughout. Therefore the bend will be over the leading leg, and the middle of the loop – the turn to the outside – will actually be in counter canter.

This is the simplest form of counter canter. You can start by making a loop just 1.5 m (5 ft) or 2 m (6 ft) in from the track, later progressing to 3 m

(10 ft), 4 m (13 ft) or 5 m (16 ft) loops when the horse understands what he has to do.

The secret of riding these loops is to make the turns gradual and smooth. If they are too sharp the horse is much more likely to lose his balance and also his correct canter lead.

## SERPENTINES

As well as circles, half-circles and loops, serpentines can be used for suppling work. A serpentine is a series of half-oval loops across the length of the arena. It starts at either C or A and finishes at A or C. Each loop takes you to the long side of the arena, back across the arena, crossing the centre line at a right angle to the opposite long side and then back again. In a 20 m (22 yd) × 40 m (44 yd) arena, a serpentine usually has three loops. In the long arena it can have

73

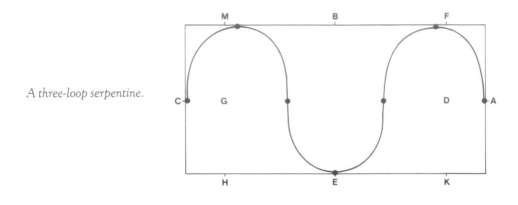

*A three-loop serpentine.*

any number of loops up to six. Serpentines with an odd number of loops (three or five) bring you out on the same rein as you started on. If the number of loops is even you will finish on the other rein.

## Three-loop serpentine

To ride a really accurate three-loop serpentine, mark out points in the arena before you mount. Divide the centre line into three equal lengths, and mark the end of each length with an obvious mark. (Use your foot to do this, so it will be visible from the horse.) This is where you will cross the centre line. Then divide the long side into six equal lengths and mark the end of the first and the fifth length (see diagram). These are the points where you will touch the long side. On the other long side you will only touch the track once and that will be at the half marker B or E.

From these markings you should be able to see the beginning, middle and end of each loop. Remember that when you cross the centre line you should be straight for at least a stride, parallel to the short sides of the arena. When you touch the long side you should be straight for at least a stride on the track.

## Riding the serpentine in rising trot

When riding a serpentine in rising trot, change your diagonal each time that you cross the centre line. If you find, however, that changing your diagonal causes a loss of balance or concentration, it is better to practise without changing and concentrate on making smooth loops. When you are more confident about the shape of the figure you are riding, you will be able to change diagonals without upset.

## Riding the serpentine in canter

When riding a serpentine in canter, the second loop will either have to be ridden in counter canter or the canter lead will have to be changed through a simple change on both occasions that you cross the centre line. Counter canter on a serpentine is quite a difficult exercise and should only be attempted if both horse and rider are confident in simpler exercises in counter canter.

When initially trying this, make the first and third loops smaller, leaving more room for the middle loop of counter canter. As soon as it can be ridden easily this way, make the loops the correct size again.

If you do the simple changes instead of the counter canter, they can be through either trot or walk. If through trot, you will find that there is very little time in which to make your transitions, so I prefer to do them through walk. The downwards transition must be well-prepared and should take place before reaching the centre line. The upwards transition should take place after crossing the centre line. Make sure that you do not lose the shape of the serpentine during these transitions.

## USE OF REINS IN TESTS

There are two more movements which you will find in Novice tests, both concerning the reins.

### Reins in one hand

If the test requires you to ride for a short period with the reins in one hand, the reins should be held in the outside hand while your inside hand hangs down by your hip as unobtrusively as possible.

### Giving the reins

'Give and retake the reins' and 'stroke the horse's neck' are movements designed to show whether your horse can stay in balance for a few strides without the help of the reins. These movements are usually asked for on the diagonal, on the long side or on a large circle.

They do not have to be performed precisely at the marker but at an unspecified point between two markers. This gives you ample time to make sure that your horse is in balance and to make an extra half-halt if necessary, before you give the reins.

You should run your hands up the horse's neck until the reins are looped and you no longer have contact with the horse's mouth. Do not bring your body forwards, though, as this will upset your balance. You must not alter your grip on the reins or let them out or you will be caught with them too long after the movement. Leave your hands forwards in this position for four or five strides, and then carefully bring them back to the ordinary position, taking care not to snatch the contact too abruptly.

While the rein contact is loose, the horse should not quicken or alter the length of his stride. He may gradually start to lower his head and neck but he should not poke his nose or raise his head.

# CHAPTER 10

# AN INTRODUCTION TO LATERAL WORK

When a horse is 'straight', his hind legs follow directly behind his forelegs. In lateral work, he moves his body sideways as well as forwards, with his hind legs and forelegs making different tracks.

Lateral work is good for developing collection and suppleness. The horse has to bring his hind legs further under his body in order to carry him sideways. This increases the engagement of his hind quarters and thus improves his balance.

Before lateral work can be ridden productively, the horse must be established in his three paces, staying straight and balanced throughout his work and being supple enough to bend when required. He must accept

and be responsive to the aids. It is particularly important that he does not run away from the leg aids, because it is these which will be asking him to move sideways.

Previous chapters have explained that the horse moves forwards from the leg, and that a crooked horse can be straightened by using the leg opposite to the direction in which he must move. The left leg asks him to move to the right, and the right leg asks him to move to the left.

When these sideways-asking leg aids are combined with supporting aids from the other leg, directions from the reins and appropriate positioning of the body, the horse can move sideways uniformly. In other words,

*Horse moving on different tracks – lateral work.*

*Horse moving straight.*

each step gains the same amount of ground forwards and the same amount of ground sideways as the previous step.

The degree of sideways movement in lateral work is called the 'angle'. The more sideways you are travelling, the less forwards you will be travelling and the angle is said to be steep. If you travel only a little sideways but quite a lot forwards, the angle is small. When horse and rider are learning lateral work, the angle should be small, which will make the movement as easy as possible while learning.

## THE LATERAL MOVEMENTS

*The turn on the forehand* is the simplest introduction to lateral work. It is a movement that you probably perform frequently in your everyday riding without realizing it – for example, to open a gate. As a schooling movement, however, it is not quite so easy! All you are doing is turning your horse around to face in the opposite direction, not by pulling him round, but by turning him with your leg so that his quarters move in a semi-circle around his forehand – hence the name 'turn on the forehand'.

The next stage is *leg yielding*, where the horse moves sideways and forward down the length of the arena, giving *you* the feeling of working on more than one track.

It is a natural progression to *shoulder-in*, which is similar to leg yielding, but requires more bend. Shoulder-in is one of the most important exercises in dressage training. It improves collection and suppleness and further develops the relationship between your inside leg and outside rein.

*Shoulder-fore* is much like shoulder-in but with a smaller angle. It is a valuable exercise to straighten the horse and to prepare him for other movements.

*Travers, half-pass* and *renvers* are lateral movements in which the horse must bend in the direction in which he is travelling. These are quite different to the previous exercises, and the need for an 'inside leg/outside rein' connection is even greater. The horse must move away from the outside leg, but bend around the inside leg.

*Travers* is also known as haunches-in and leads on to *half-pass*, for which the aids and the movement are exactly the same. The difference is that travers is ridden on the track or the centre line with the haunches in, whereas half-pass is ridden sideways across from the track to the centre line or vice-versa. Travers is more of a training exercise than a show-piece, while half-pass is a very attractive movement to watch, especially when it is performed all the way across the arena.

*Renvers* is similar to travers and half-pass. The degree of sideways movement and bend are the same, but the quarters stay on the track, the forehand comes in and the horse is bent to the outside.

The *half-pirouette* is a 180-degree turn where the horse moves his forehand in a half-circle around his hind quarters. If performed from a halt, it is called a *turn on the haunches*. Half-pirouettes are performed in walk and, when the horse has achieved a high degree of collection, in canter.

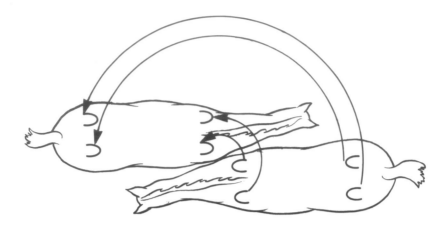

*A turn on the forehand to the left.*

In all lateral work, you need to be patient and restrict yourself to learning one movement at a time. Don't try to teach your horse too much on the same day – you will almost certainly confuse him and probably yourself as well.

## TURN ON THE FOREHAND

The turn on the forehand is best ridden from a halt to begin with, and later from walk. Make your halt a little away from the track so that the horse has room to turn without banging his nose on the fence. The halt should be square and well-balanced, and the horse should remain alert and on the bit.

If he has put himself into 'neutral' and switched off, then wake him up by walking on and making another halt. This time keep him on your aids with a light leg and rein contact.

To begin a turn to the right, ask for a little flexion to the right, weight your right seat bone a little more and use your right leg just behind the girth to ask the horse to move sideways. As soon as he reacts to the leg, relax it for a moment. Then ask for the next step in the same way until you can make the full turn with a light press–release–press–release of the leg.

Keep your left leg passive to start with or the horse may not understand which leg he has to move away from. Then use it on the girth to maintain activity in the walk or to ride forwards a step if he moves too much to the left or backwards. Use your left rein to control the speed with little checks and to prevent his left shoulder from escaping to the left.

When the turn is complete, ride straight forwards and praise him. Never halt when you finish because this will block the energy that you have just created in the turn and cause tension.

Remember that the forehand is not just a pivot point. The forelegs must move in walk rhythm, marking time on the spot or in a tiny semi-circle.

## Take it steady

If your horse is young, tense or excitable, it is best to make only a quarter-turn on the forehand to start with. Take the turn step by step, rewarding him for each correct move. Make several turns one way and be sure that they are understood before you attempt one the other way. If you have a lot of problems with the turn in one direction, continue working quietly at it and leave the other direction until another day.

A light tap with the whip can be used to reinforce the inside leg if necessary. Always be careful not to restrict the horse with your hands because this may result in him running backwards.

If at any time during the turn you feel that he has 'frozen' himself to the spot, ride him forwards for a few steps and then try again. Remember that it is not an exercise to turn him around as fast as possible but to teach him to move away from your leg in rhythmical sideways steps.

## LEG YIELDING

In leg yielding, the horse moves sideways and forwards down the length of the arena, with his body parallel to the long side, and a slight flexion at the poll, away from the direction in which he is travelling.

To start leg yielding choose the direction in which you found a turn on the forehand easiest. For example, let us suppose that your horse moves more easily away from your left leg. Going large on the left rein, ride past

A and turn on to the 5 m (6fl yd) line (halfway between the centre line and the track). Go straight for a few strides, prepare him with a half-halt, and ask for a slight flexion to the left. Then use your left leg just behind the girth to push him sideways towards the track. Keep your right leg on the girth and use it to maintain the forwards movement. Use your right rein to check the forward movement if necessary and to prevent the right shoulder from escaping ahead of the quarters.

The aids themselves are simple, but making corrections when something goes wrong is more difficult. There are several ways in which the horse may try to evade you. In the above example, if he ignores your left leg and walks straight forwards, check with the right rein and use your left leg a little more strongly, or reinforce it with the whip. If he rushes sideways with his forehand but leaves the quarters trailing, slow him down and move your hands to the left. This should keep the right shoulder under control while your left leg moves his quarters over until his body is parallel to the track again.

An important part of the leg-yielding exercise is to be sure that at any time you can walk straight forwards using, in this case, your right leg. It is a good exercise to do a few steps of leg yielding and then a few steps straight, then a few more steps of leg yielding and then straight again. In this way you achieve better control and keep your horse on the aids.

In the early stages a few steps sideways in walk are satisfactory. When you find it easy to leg yield from the 5 m (6fl yd) line to the track, try from the centre line to the track or

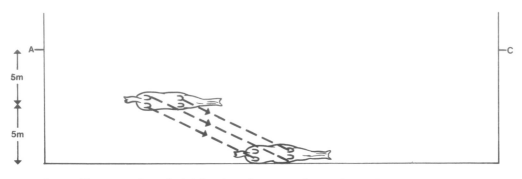

*Leg yielding away from the left leg, from the 5 metre line to the track.*

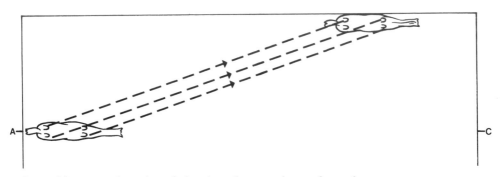

*Leg yielding away from the right leg, from the centre line to the track.*

vice-versa. Then repeat the exercise in trot, coming back to walk if you find it difficult to stay in control in trot.

A common fault in leg yielding (and, later, in shoulder-in) is an exaggerated neck bend. This causes the horse to fall sideways on to his outside shoulder, rather than moving uniformly sideways in balance. This can be corrected by straightening the horse and making sure that he moves sideways from the leg.

## SHOULDER-IN AND SHOULDER-FORE

The angle for shoulder-in is measured by the horse's position in relation to the long-side track. When viewed from behind, the horse should be travelling down the track with his forehand in, at an angle of about 30 degrees to the track, with an inside bend. He should be on three tracks – his outside hind leg makes one track, his inside hind leg and outside foreleg make the next track and the inside foreleg makes the innermost track. If the shoulder-in has too great an angle, the horse would be on four tracks instead of three.

Shoulder-fore is a direct translation from the German 'Schulter vor', meaning that the horse is positioned with his shoulder a little to the inside and has a slight bend to the inside. In shoulder-fore the angle is less than that for shoulder-in. The inside foreleg is just in from the track, and the outside foreleg is on a track between the tracks of the two hind legs. Shoulder-fore can be ridden in walk, trot or canter. It is a good exercise to straighten the horse if he is crooked, with his quarters in. The aids for shoulder fore are the same as those for shoulder-in, but you ask for less angle and less bend.

For shoulder-in, the inside leg is on the girth, asking the horse to move sideways and to maintain bend and impulsion. The outside rein controls the speed and the angle and contains the impulsion. The inside rein should receive the bend that is created by the inside leg. The contact should remain light and elastic throughout. The outside leg is behind the girth to control the quarters.

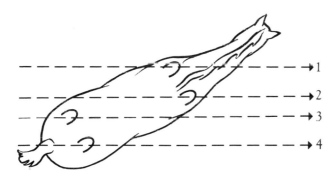

*Hoofprints of shoulder-in left – on three tracks.*

*On four tracks – incorrect.*

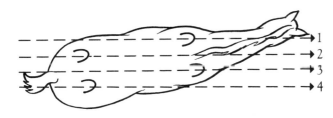

*Shoulder-fore – less angle than shoulder-in.*

Pay particular attention to your position in shoulder-in. Unless you sit correctly the horse will *not* be able to bring his shoulder in. Your body should face in the same direction as your horse's body. Keep your shoulders and hips in line with his, weight your inside seat bone slightly but do *not* lean inwards or forwards. Your head should be erect and you should look between your horse's ears (although you will need to glance down the track from time to time to ensure that you stay on one line and do not drift). If your body points straight down the track, your horse will move straight down the track instead of being in shoulder-in.

### Starting shoulder-in, in walk

To start shoulder in, the horse should be in collected or medium walk, and he should be attentive to your aids. Use the short side of the arena to prepare, then ask for an inside bend in the corner. Half-halt as you come out of the corner. Turn yourself and the horse as if you were going to ride across the diagonal line. As he starts to leave the track, however, check his forward movement with your outside rein and use your inside leg on the girth to push him sideways down the track. Weight your inside seat bone a little more too.

The horse must be positioned in such a way that you *could* ride forwards diagonally across the arena at the beginning – but by checking with your outside rein and pushing with your inside leg you achieve shoulder-in instead.

It is better for the angle to be too small rather than too steep in the early stages. The horse must maintain his

rhythm, balance and outline, and too steep an angle may cause him to lose one or all of these.

When the horse has done several satisfactory steps of shoulder-in take his shoulder back to the track and straighten up. To do this, turn your body so that you are facing down the track and ride straight forwards with both legs into an even rein contact.

You may wonder why you should not ride forwards across the arena, instead of straightening up on to the track. In fact, you may do either, but if you straighten up on to the track it will discourage the horse from drifting in off the track *during* the shoulder-in. In more advanced training, when the shoulder-in is well established, it can be used as a preparation for medium or extended trot. The shoulder-in improves collection and suppleness and therefore gives the horse more freedom and expression in his medium trot. *Then* he can be ridden out of the shoulder-in straight across the diagonal line into medium trot.

When you have established shoulder-in on the track, try it on the centre line or the 5 m (6 yd) line, both of which are a good test of your control. You may find that you need more outside leg when there is no wall or fence to stop you drifting outwards. Remember that the horse's hind feet should be on the centre line, or 5 m (6 yd) line, and his forefeet should be to the inside.

A common fault is for the hind quarters to fall outwards rather than the shoulder coming in. This should be corrected by bringing the hind quarters on to the line or track again, with the outside leg, and then by bringing the shoulder in off the line or

*Positioning the horse for travers to the right.*

track as normal.

In competitions, shoulder-in is included in tests at Elementary level and above and is usually performed at collected trot. In training start in walk (this gives you more time to make corrections) before progressing to trot. Try shoulder-fore as an introduction to shoulder-in in trot, or in canter; to keep the horse straight.

## TRAVERS

So far, all the lateral work has involved some degree of bend or flexion away from the direction in which the horse is moving. From now on all the movements require bend in the direction in which the horse is moving.

You need very good control of your

legs, using the outside leg behind the girth to create the sideways motion and the inside leg close to the girth to create the bend and the forward momentum. The inside leg has to be firm enough to keep the horse bent around it, but not tight or squeezing because this would stop the sideways movement that the other leg is creating.

Travers is ridden on the long side or the centre line, with the haunches to the inside and the forehand on the original line. The legs should make four tracks: outside fore, inside fore, outside hind and inside hind on the innermost track. It requires control and co-ordination, so try it in walk first, and later in collected trot.

To prepare for the travers, check that the horse is on the aids and that you can bend him to the inside. You will need about the same amount of bend as you would have on an 8 m (26 ft) circle. Use your inside leg in the corner to get the bend before starting on the long side. I like to shorten my inside rein before starting, so that I can keep the bend without having to draw my hand back or across the neck.

Don't ride too deep into the corner – this will make it more difficult to bring the hind quarters in off the

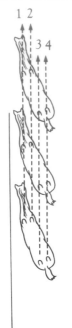

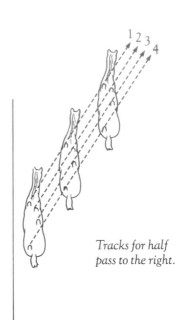

*Tracks for travers
to the right.*

*Tracks for half
pass to the right.*

track. Instead, cut the corner slightly and when you are halfway around it don't keep turning but stay at an angle to the track to begin your travers.

The outside rein and outside leg dictate the angle of the travers. The outside rein is used outwards – away from the neck – to position the forehand. The outside leg is behind the girth to keep the quarters in and ask the horse to move sideways down the track. These aids must be light and quick enough that they do not block the bend to the inside. The inside leg on the girth maintains impulsion and bend, and the inside rein receives the bend created by the leg.

Your body should be turned to face the same direction as the horse's body is facing – about 30 degrees to the wall. Keep your outside shoulder and hip well back. Weight your inside seat bone a little more and keep your seat in the middle of the saddle. It is easy to slip to the outside without realizing.

Glance down the track every few strides, but do not lose your position.

To increase the angle, turn your body more to the outside, check with the outside rein and use more outside leg. To decrease the angle, turn your body more to the inside, use your inside leg to drive the horse forwards and relax your outside leg.

When you are confident with the travers in walk, start it in trot, but be prepared to walk again if you have difficulties. If you do travers on the centre line, picture the line as a wall that you must stay behind.

When the horse is well-established in travers, try riding the first half of the long side in shoulder-in, then ride an 8 m (26 ft) circle, and finish the long side in travers.

## HALF-PASS

Half-pass is exactly the same as travers, but instead of travelling down the track at an angle, the horse travels sideways and forwards across the arena, parallel to the long side. You can use the same aids as with travers, but try to imagine a line diagonally across the arena, and ride travers along this line. This helps you to keep a uniform sideways and forwards movement. Try it in walk first.

To start half-pass, turn down the centre line (for example, to the left) from Λ. If you need extra time to prepare and to work on the bend, make a 10 m (11 yd) circle left at D. Then imagine that there is a wall from D to H (if necessary dismount and draw yourself a line on the ground) and that you are going to ride travers down the track next to this wall.

If you find yourself creeping over the line, you are travelling too much forwards and not enough sideways. In that case, you will need to reinforce your outside leg and rein aids to decrease the forwards movement and increase the sidewards movement.

The horse's body should be parallel to the long side. If his quarters are trailing a little, it does not really matter to start with. If his quarters are leading, however, he will not be able to move freely across and his strides will become short and restricted. Nevertheless, do not allow the quarters to trail more and more towards the end or you will eventually lose the bend and the sideways movement. A neat beginning and end to the half-pass are essential.

The forehand should lead a little in the first stride. Starting from a shoulder-in position gives a fluent start to the half-pass and is a good way to ensure that the horse is bent correctly around your inside leg.

If the horse anticipates the start of the half-pass by throwing his quarters in, you should correct him and prepare him by riding a few steps of shoulder-fore. Do not start the half-pass until you are absolutely in control. You may need to start again from the turn at A if your correction has taken you more than halfway down the centre line.

The half-pass can also be performed from the beginning of the long side, finishing on the centre line. This is better in that you can choose which way to turn when you finish. You can go back on the same rein if necessary and do it again. If you do it from the centre line to the track, you finish on the other rein and will have to change before repeating it.

Don't try to work on both half-passes simultaneously. Finish your work on one and, when you are satisfied, try the other rein. If, however, you have spent ages trying to overcome problems on one rein, leave the other one until another day.

Half-pass is required in tests at Medium level upwards in trot and in canter. Half-pass at canter requires a well-balanced canter with a degree of collection. If the canter is too free or the strides are long and laboured, the horse will not have sufficient spring to carry him forwards and sideways and may fall into trot. Canter half-pass is best performed from the long side to the centre line so that you can stay on the same leg. If you do it from the centre to the track, make sure that you arrive at the track well before the corner so that you can either make a simple change or prepare for the corner, staying in counter canter.

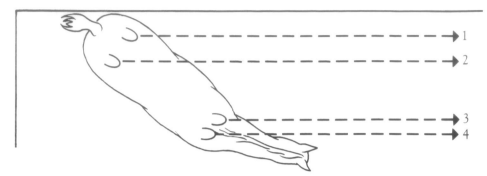

*In renvers to the left, the horse travels clockwise around the arena, with his forehand in and his quarters on the track. He is bent to the left and travels on three or four tracks, depending on the angle.*

## RENVERS

Renvers is the same for the horse as travers or half-pass; however, it is more difficult to ride because of where it is performed. The positioning of the horse's body is similar to shoulder-in, but the bend is to the outside and the horse should be on four tracks rather than three.

To start renvers left, bring the forehand in off the track as for shoulder-in, then ask for a left bend. Bring your right leg back and your left leg forwards, weight your left seat bone slightly more and shorten your left rein; alternatively, ride renvers on the centre line – it requires greater control but is easier to start.

## HALF-PIROUETTE

The half-pirouette is a turn through 180 degrees, where the hind feet make a small half-circle almost on the spot and the forefeet make a larger half-circle around the hind feet. It is performed in walk (and later canter), with the horse bent slightly to the inside. A regular four-beat walk should be maintained throughout.

Your aids need to be well-coordinated and you must ride your horse forwards into the bridle throughout. Bend him in the direction of the turn and do not allow him to step backwards at all.

Starting the half-pirouette on the track, the forehand turns to the

*A half-pirouette to the left.*

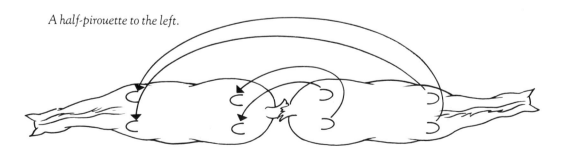

inside. The hind quarters stay on or close to the track and the forehand makes a larger half-circle around the quarters. The radius of the circle will be equal to the distance between the horse's hind legs and forelegs. Finish on the track but facing in the opposite direction.

Prepare with a half-halt, weight your inside seat bone a little more and bring the forehand off the track, as for shoulder-fore. This gives the horse an indication of where he will have to turn and ensures that the quarters are not leading at the beginning (important because otherwise the half-pirouette will become too big).

Use your outside leg behind the girth to turn him, alternating with your inside leg on the girth to keep the activity. Use your outside rein to control the degree of the turn and the speed, and your inside rein to indicate the direction of the movement and control the bend.

Keep your hips and shoulders parallel to those of the horse, look between his ears and be careful not to get left behind the movement. Be sure to keep the horse turning actively. His legs must keep the rhythm and sequence of the walk; if the hind legs become 'stuck' the horse will pivot and lose his balance.

**A half-pirouette to the right in walk.**

# CHAPTER 11

# PREPARING FOR A COMPETITION

Competing is a good way to check the progress of your training. In a four- or five-minute test you will bring together everything that you and your horse have learned. This means that the test you choose must be appropriate to the stage of training and well within your own and your horse's capabilities. There are six levels of test, starting at Preliminary and progressing through Novice and Elementary all the way up to Advanced.

Preliminary involves walk, trot and canter on both reins with some simple turns and circles. When you can master these with smooth, obedient transitions between the paces, you will be ready for your first test. Preparing for the test will expose any weaknesses on which you may need to concentrate.

## THE IMPORTANCE OF GOOD PREPARATION

If you have not competed in dressage competitions before, your first test can be quite nerve-racking. Good preparation will ensure that you have a trouble-free and enjoyable day.

Dressage is becoming more and more popular and there are plenty of competitions from which to choose.

To compete in affiliated competitions, you and your horse need to be registered with the British Horse Society Dressage Group. You will get a schedule listing all the affiliated competitions in every part of the country.

Although many Preliminary classes are included, tests at this level are unaffiliated and you should make enquiries at local riding clubs, riding schools or livery yards to find out about unaffiliated shows. Schedules can usually be found in your feed merchants' or saddlers', and they are sometimes advertised in the local press. As a member of the BHS Dressage Group, you would also receive a rule book and regular newsletters.

Even if you don't plan to register your horse at first, it is a good idea to join the BHS Dressage Group. Most unaffiliated shows are run under BHS rules so you will need a copy of the rulebook and copies of the tests, all of which can be obtained from the BHS. New tests are written every year and older ones are updated or made redundant. When you enter a class make sure that you have a copy of the right test and check that the year the test was written corresponds to the one in the schedule.

## Your first test

For your first outing, choose a small, friendly, local show where you will know a few faces. It is important that you and the horse enjoy the day. It should be a quiet introduction for you both to see what it is all about. You must, of course, ride and look your very best, but don't expect to win! Aim to go home with the satisfaction of having done your best and having shown that your horse is well-trained so far.

See that your horse's flu vaccination is up-to-date; some shows will ask you to produce a valid certificate before competing. Your horse should not be shod too near to the show date, since newly shod feet can make a horse a bit 'footy', especially if the ground is hard, and he may not move as freely as usual. On the other hand, worn shoes will give less grip and may not be secure. So, if he is due for shoeing, arrange to have him shod a week before, and remember to ask for stud holes if you need them.

## PRACTISING THE TEST

Once your entry has been accepted and you have a copy of the test, you must set about learning it, so that the order of movements is clearly fixed in your mind. In most competitions you are allowed a 'commander' to call your test in the competition.

Read the test very carefully before you go through it. Find out exactly where you have to make transitions. In canter these may be anywhere between two markers, but into walk and trot the transitions are usually at a specific marker. This doesn't mean they have to be performed abruptly at the marker; on the contrary, they should be smooth and progressive. You should aim to make the transition as your body is level with the marker, so plenty of preparation is needed.

You must show that you have a correct basic position and can ride the horse sympathetically and effectively through the required movements. The horse must show true and regular paces, moving forwards and straight into a steady rein contact in a round outline. The picture of horse and rider should be one of a happy partnership and sound basic work, which will form the foundations for further training. What the judge does not want to see at this level (or indeed at any level) is that the horse has been forced or restricted, either in his paces or his outline, or that he is clearly not ready for the test.

## Entry, halt and salute

Every dressage test starts with an entry at A, down the centre line and a halt and salute, usually at X. First impressions are very important so practise riding down the centre line in trot without halting until you can stay absolutely straight on the line, from either direction. Then try making the halt at X; use several half-halts before reaching X to make sure that you are in control.

If the horse is really waiting for you and not rushing along with ideas of his own, you should be able to ride him forwards into the halt with your legs. This will keep him in better balance during the halt and make the move-off easier. Your legs will also help keep him straight and help him make a squarer halt.

If you have difficulty stopping at X and have to pull quite hard into the halt, this will lead to many problems – crookedness, tension, resistance and fidgeting in the halt. Get to the root of the problem before the horse makes a habit of rushing down the centre line.

Practise riding down the centre line, and make several transitions to walk and to halt. Repeat this until the horse responds willingly every time and then try the entry, halt and move-off. The move-off should be straight, with the horse moving energetically forwards towards C. Prepare for your turn by asking for a slight flexion in the required direction. This will give the horse and the judge confidence that you know which way you are going to turn.

The salute should be a simple, neat, unhurried movement involving one arm and your head. You should not lift your seat out of the saddle and make a bow – this not only looks dreadful, but it also upsets your balance. Now that many people sensibly wear a hat with a chin strap, it is not compulsory for a man to take his hat off when saluting. When the horse is settled in halt, look straight at the judge and smile (do not grin). Put your reins and whip (if carried) in one hand, preferably your left hand, although there are no hard and fast rules about which hand it should be. Drop your right hand down by your right hip, with the back of your hand facing the judge and your fingers pointing downwards, then nod your head slowly down and up again. Put your right hand back on the rein but do not rush straight off into trot.

Count to three and then move off and start your test, taking each movement at a time, and giving your full concentration to every step.

## Familiarity with the movements

As the day of the show approaches, plan your work schedule so that you will have practised the test a few times. It is vital that you are familiar with all the movements and how to ride them, and in doing this you will also learn how your horse may try to evade you in some movements. You must stay one step ahead of him and make sure that he doesn't have a chance to get away with anything.

You may find that your horse starts to anticipate the next movement if you ride the test too many times. If this happens check that you really have him on the aids and under control. He may be doing what he thinks the next movement will be simply because you have not made it clear to him what the next movement really is.

If you still find that he is anticipating, ride the test one movement at a time. Between each movement walk and make a circle in walk, which will enable you to keep him between leg and hand and prevent him from trying to rush into the next movement.

The most usual place that horses will anticipate is after the free walk on a long rein; as you pick up the reins, they start to jog or trot. Try halting every time you pick up the reins from free walk, so that he starts to associate picking up the reins with stopping rather than with rushing off. When you do this in the test, the horse will be expecting to have to stop and you will be able to keep your leg on and push him forwards to keep walking, without any worry about jogging.

## SADDLERY AND DRESS

Find out the rules about saddlery and dress. A simple snaffle bridle should be used at Preliminary level, but check what bits and nosebands the rules permit you to use. If the one that you normally use is not allowed, you will have to find another. Avoid *any* last minute changes.

A white numnah is smarter than a coloured one, although black is acceptable on a grey horse. A saddle-shaped numnah is suitable, although if your horse has a long back a square numnah will make a good picture. Whatever numnah you use, make sure that it is secure so that it doesn't slip or wrinkle.

If you use a coloured girth, as opposed to a leather one, it should be either white or a colour which will look unobtrusive on your horse's coat. Red, yellow or blue girths are not suitable in the dressage arena. Brightly coloured reins or browbands also look out-of-place.

For the rider, at Preliminary level a tweed coat should be worn, with either a tie or a correctly tied hunting stock and pin. White stocks should only be worn with a navy or black coat, so choose another colour to match your tweed coat and wear a sober-coloured shirt underneath. 'Buttonholes' are not worn for dressage. Gloves are compulsory, as of course is a hat.

Your hair should be tidy underneath the hat, with *no* fringe showing under the peak. Girls with long hair should wear a hairnet or a long plait and then double this up with a ponytail band or something similar so that there is not a huge net of hair bouncing around halfway down their backs looking untidy.

*Untidy hair can spoil an otherwise perfect turnout.*

*Neatly tied back hair, staying close to the rim of the hat at the back with no wispy bits hanging out.*

91

**Horse and rider correctly turned out for a Preliminary or Novice Dressage test.**

## TURNOUT OF THE HORSE

The appearance of your horse is not marked, but the tidier he is the better the first impression as you enter the arena. If it is winter and he is clipped, make sure that it is a tidy, even clip; unlevel lines may make him look an unbalanced shape.

His mane should be plaited if possible. A well-pulled mane is much easier to plait than a long, bushy one, so if you need to pull it do so a week before you need to plait it. I prefer a plaited forelock, but you *can* leave it loose.

Pulled or plaited tails look best, but if your horse violently objects to both of these, bandage his tail regularly to make it look neater. Make sure the bottom of the tail is cut so that it hangs level when carried.

Heels look neater if they are trimmed. This also applies to the chin and underneath of the jaw.

## ARRIVAL AT THE COMPETITION

When you arrive (preferably at least an hour before you intend to start riding) report to the secretary, and collect your number if necessary. Check the time of your test, which arena you are in, where you can warm up and whether you have to report to an arena steward. Watch one or two other competitors if your class has already started. This will give you an idea of how the arena rides and what signal the judge uses for you to start. It will also remind you of the test.

When you and the horse are ready, mount and walk about quietly to let him absorb the atmosphere. This walking will help him relax after the journey before you expect him to work harder. When you start to work him, find enough space to work on a 20m (22yd) circle. Be careful not to let your circle get bigger and bigger, but discipline yourself to ride as if you were in an arena.

This preparation period is very important and needs your full concentration if you are to perform well in the arena. You must earn the horse's trust and respect by riding him consistently and working him as you would at home.

Ride plenty of transitions and practise each of the movements that you will have to ride in the test individually. Try to avoid movements which may confuse the horse for the test.

Keep an eye on the steward and check whether the class is running to time or not. Allow a few minutes to take brushing boots off and apply extra fly repellent if necessary.

When the competitor before you finishes his or her test, start riding around the outside of the arena. Show your number to the judge's 'writer', who will usually be sitting on the passenger side of the car. Ride quietly around the arena until you are given the signal to start. In these crucial moments before you start your test,

never practise what you do badly; instead show off what you do well.

## RIDING THE TEST

Enter the arena on whichever rein you have found to be easiest in practice. Once in the arena you must show the judge how well you have trained your horse. The judge will be marking from the moment you enter the arena at 'A' until the final salute. He or she will do this from a position at 'C' and will usually sit in a car with the 'writer', who records the marks for each movement as well as any comments that the judge may make.

'Collective marks' are awarded for the correctness of the paces and general way of going, and for your position and effectiveness. The judge will usually make a few constructive comments beside these. At the end of the class the marks will all be added up to produce a winner.

Riding a test requires enormous concentration from both horse and rider. During one of my first Elementary tests, at the age of 12, a riderless horse galloped through my arena. I was thinking so hard about the test that I did not quite realize what was happening and managed to continue the test without a pause. The unexpected excitement generated some outstanding impulsion in my pony and we won the class! But the real lesson from this experience is that competitors in other arenas, who were a bit quicker on the uptake, halted to allow the runaway through; they then had immense difficulty regaining the attention and concentration of their mounts.

I learned from this episode that

whatever happens you must keep going. Even if you make a terrible mistake, continue with the test. Each movement counts towards a different mark. You could get 0 out of 10 by, for example, going outside the arena boards, but if you are back within the boards and going well, there is no reason why you couldn't get a 7 for the next movement.

When you finish your test, leave the arena at free walk on a long rein at A. Remember that the judge is still watching you until you are out of the arena. Even if your test was not perfect, make much of your horse. Walk him until he is cool and relaxed before returning to the box; make sure he is comfortable before you see to your own needs.

By the time you have finished this, your mark will probably be on the scoreboard. When the class has finished, you will be able to collect your sheet, which will show the judge's marks and comments. Read these carefully and learn what you can about how your performance could have been better. Attend the prize-giving, even if you were not a winner, and thank the secretary or organizer of the competition before you leave.

Competing should be fun and challenging for both you and your horse. Good preparation and a calm approach will make a vital contribution to you and your horse's enjoyment of the day.

# INDEX

Page numbers in *italic* refer to the illustrations